"E. K. Strawser helps the church refocus our atten̲̅ ̲̅ ̲̅ ̲̅ on real discipleship. This book is for deep thinkers who want to see Christians focus on wnat really matters to God with regard to who the church is and how to act that out well in today's world. Strawser is well practiced and passionate about what she teaches here."

Linda Bergquist, church planting catalyst for the North American Mission Board and coauthor of *City Shaped Churches*

"Whether you're planting, re-missioning, or recalibrating a church, *Centering Discipleship* is a field guide and compass all in one. This book is practical and tested in real communities looking to make disciples for the sake of God's mission, and it is a tool that helps us to chart a path when the old maps no longer work. With surgical precision and humility, Eun Strawser helps us unmask the problems that keep us stuck and imagine how our churches can disciple their way into the future."

Josh Hayden, author of *Sacred Hope* and senior pastor of First Baptist Church Ashland

"Discipleship is often misunderstood and left undone in the American church today. But Eun Strawser, drawing on her wealth of wisdom gained from on-the-ground experience leading and discipling missional communities, serves as a wonderful guide for the rest of us in crafting our own contextualized pathways—not another cookie-cutter program or curriculum to implement uncritically—for following Jesus in mission and in transformation where God has called us. This is a rich resource, grounded in missional theology and full of practical wisdom, essential for everyone who dreams of the church as the community of the kingdom on mission and desires to join the work of seeing the dream realized."

Kyuboem Lee, director and associate professor of missiology at Missio Seminary

"In the contemporary life of the local church, discipleship has become paramount. Eun Strawser has taken the complex and challenging ministerial phenomenon and converted it into a wonderful array of practical applications that would be helpful for any church regardless of context. I was totally impressed by the way she handled discipleship pathways by utilizing the progression of past recipes to local cuisine. The chapter on the four spaces as they relate to discipleship in culture is definitely my favorite in terms of ease of language and ease of use. I know that many churches will be blessed by Eun's handling of this much-needed dialogue and modeling."

Wayne D. Faison, senior pastor of East End Baptist Church and executive director of the Baptist General Association of Virginia

"Eun Strawser is passionate about putting discipleship at the front and center of all we do as God's people. And her book *Centering Discipleship* bears testimony that when a church gets serious about really following Jesus, everything changes. This practical book is both compelling, as it is rooted in a lived story, and impressive, as it suggests practical ways to make this happen in your church."

Debra Hirsch, cofounder of Forge Mission Training Network and author of *Redeeming Sex*

"*Centering Discipleship* is a masterful book that powerfully illuminates the essentials of disciplemaking. By calling readers out of programs and into contextualized pathways that create lasting and vital transformation, Eun Strawser offers the keys to creating not only mature Jesus-followers but also movements of disciples. Read this brilliant book and put Eun's decades of learning and wisdom into practice."

Lisa Rodriguez-Watson, national director of Missio Alliance

"*Centering Discipleship* is a powerful handbook for any leader who wants to escape consumer models of Christianity and help their church pursue the Great Commission. Both erudite and practical, with years of experience, E. K. Strawser describes how to design adaptable, biblical, Jesus-shaped pathways of discipleship and evaluate their effectiveness. She reveals how to identify where church communities function in an unbiblical way and how to address these issues so discipleship can become central. Strawser shows how to implement the practices she has developed so that disciples produce disciples and a growing community begins to multiply. Highly recommended!"

Paul Maconochie, team leader for Uptick with the Baptist General Association of Virginia

"E. K. Strawser's book *Centering Discipleship* is relevant and prophetic. In the Western world, modern church growth has unfortunately become identified by an increase in numbers, while discipleship is a catchy phrase with limited emphasis in the life of the congregation. No wonder: discipleship is hard work and requires patience, perseverance, and time. Strawser's stories about how she implemented the five discipleship core essentials should be an encouragement to any pastoral team committed to the same principles that Jesus used in his ministry to develop his disciples. I hope that many church leaders will read this book and determine how to contextualize these principles in their own setting."

Kathy H. Dudley, founder and president of Imani Bridges and founding member of the Christian Community Development Association

"I wish E. K. Strawser's book had been around when I first started planting churches and coaching planters twenty years ago. Strawser does something few have done: she gives a holistic, transformational, communal, Jesus-soaked vision. And she lays out the practical pathway needed for each of us to properly discover and contextualize discipleship in our specific cultural, economic, geographic, modal, vocational, and ecclesiological settings. My heart is beating faster just thinking about the disciples that will be multiplied through this work! This will be my go-to resource for church planters and leaders in years to come."

Yucan Chiu, senior director of Redeemer City to City, kingdom diversity catalyst for Stadia Church Planting, and founder of the Ethnos Network

"In this eminently practical book, E. K. Strawser gives us a crystal-clear picture of what discipleship is (and isn't) and lays out a simple rubric for developing a reproducible discipleship pathway for any context. Because she draws from her own rich, on-the-ground experience of making disciples and equipping communities for mission, Strawser has a way of making profound truths accessible and doable. This is the book I wish I'd had when I planted my first church."

Ben Sternke, author of *Having the Mind of Christ* and pastor at The Table, Indianapolis

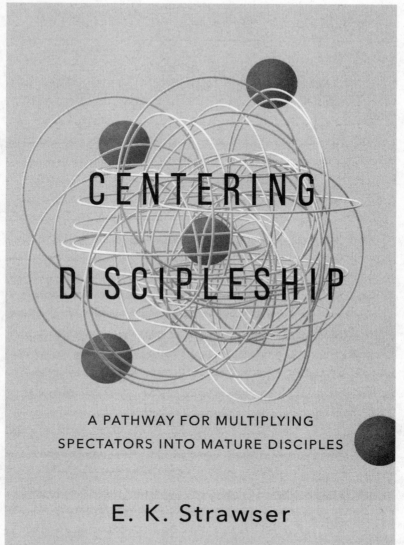

CENTERING
DISCIPLESHIP

A PATHWAY FOR MULTIPLYING
SPECTATORS INTO MATURE DISCIPLES

E. K. Strawser

Foreword by JR Woodward

An imprint of InterVarsity Press
Downers Grove, Illinois

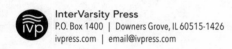

InterVarsity Press
P.O. Box 1400 | Downers Grove, IL 60515-1426
ivpress.com | email@ivpress.com

InterVarsity Press® is the publishing division of InterVarsity Christian Fellowship/USA®. For more information, visit intervarsity.org.

All Scripture quotations, unless otherwise indicated, are taken from The Holy Bible, New International Version®, NIV®. Copyright © 1973, 1978, 1984, 2011 by Biblica, Inc.™ Used by permission of Zondervan. All rights reserved worldwide. www.zondervan.com. The "NIV" and "New International Version" are trademarks registered in the United States Patent and Trademark Office by Biblica, Inc.™

While any stories in this book are true, some names and identifying information may have been changed to protect the privacy of individuals.

The publisher cannot verify the accuracy or functionality of website URLs used in this book beyond the date of publication.

Cover design: Cindy Kiple
Interior design: Jeanna Wiggins

ISBN 978-1-5140-0706-8 (print) | ISBN 978-1-5140-0707-5 (digital)

Printed in the United States of America ♾

Library of Congress Cataloging-in-Publication Data
A catalog record for this book is available from the Library of Congress.

29 28 27 26 25 24 23 | 13 12 11 10 9 8 7 6 5 4 3 2 1

DEDICATED TO

Ma Ke Alo o

Owners

who live out Presence

in more ways than

I can ever measure

Aloha pumehana

CONTENTS

FOREWORD

JR Woodward

OUR WORLD IS IN A STATE OF CHAOS. From the pandemic to the racial crises accented by the tragic death of George Floyd, from the Russian invasion of Ukraine to the rising tensions between China and the United States, we are facing difficult times. There is rising inflation and economic uncertainty. Putin is even threatening nuclear war. In *The Fourth Turning*, William Strauss and Neil Howe make the case that historically we are in the "crisis" cycle of history. Winter has arrived.

This is the time for the church to shine, to be the light of the world. Instead, the church has been complicit in racism and Christian nationalism. The number of leaders who have fallen into domineering leadership has become epidemic. We have become good at producing state-of-the-art worship services that rival Vegas shows, but we have fundamentally failed at the most basic task of the church: to *be* and *make* disciples of Jesus Christ.

While each of the Gospel writers says it differently, the sole message recorded after Jesus' resurrection and before his ascension was the Great Commission. Not only has the church lost the art of discipleship, but we have unintentionally created structures that work against our best attempts at putting discipleship in its proper place.

I've been waiting for a book that helps us concretely and creatively move discipleship from the periphery of what we do to the center. I've been waiting for a book that enables us to cultivate and contextualize a local approach to discipleship, avoiding the McDonaldization of the church. I've been waiting for a book that uncovers our assumptions about discipleship and enables us to develop a holistic discipleship pathway that is truly transformative. The wait is over! For this is exactly what *Centering Discipleship* does—and more.

Knowing E. K. Strawser and having experienced her community firsthand for over a year, I can tell you that what Strawser writes about is not just theory for her and *Ma Ke Alo o*; it is practiced reality. What you will learn in this book will be life transforming for you and those you love and lead. And if you enact the wisdom you discover, it will enable your church to join God in the renewal of your neighborhood and cultivate social good that gives witness to the good news.

Strawser equips us to develop a local discipleship pathway in light of the places where God has sent us. We are not given a prescriptive recipe that must be followed slavishly; we are taught how to cook our own recipes of discipleship. We are given the opportunity to infuse the flavor of our own local neighborhood into our discipleship pathway, which honors the places where we have been sent to minister.

But I must warn you: as you start to enact the wisdom you find in this book, you will open yourself up to *being* the church in a way that you may never have expected. But if you allow the Holy Spirit to guide you, you will taste the goodness, beauty, joy, and freedom it brings. Once you have experienced being the church in this way, you will likely never return to Egypt. While on the road to the promised land, you will feel tempted to return because of your illusions of the good life in slavery. But don't give up. When you are tempted, come back to this resource, and you will find the motivation and guidance that will enable you to move forward in cultivating communities of faith, hope, and love.

PROLOGUE

IN MARCH OF 2020, I experienced in my local church in Hawaii what the Western world and every other church experienced: the pandemic shut everything down. As we anxiously waited to see what we could or could not safely do, every entity in Hawaii instantaneously stopped operating. Kamehameha Schools, a private educational system that serves as a cultural emblem in Hawaii, canceled its long-standing and revered tradition of "Song Contest." Shutting down a society also meant shutting down a global economy. The world was hurled into an economic downturn that we are still reeling from today. On top of that, in the summer of 2020, the United States went through a cascade of racial and ethnic upheaval with the witnessed murder of George Floyd at the hands of police officers. Fall saw a heightened peak of political polarization the likes of which this generation had never experienced, and winter brought with it the death of Vicha Ratanapakdee, the rise of anti-Asian hate crimes, and the Capitol insurrection. In just one year's time, our culture changed drastically into something nearly unrecognizable.

In March of 2020, Andy Crouch, Kurt Keilhacker, and Dave Blanchard from Praxis Labs wrote a pivotal article, saying, "The priority of leaders must be to set aside confidence in their current playbook as quickly as possible, write a new one that honors their mission and the communities they serve, and make the most of their organization's assets—their people, financial capital, and social capital, leaning on relationship and trust."[1] They added, "From today onward, most leaders must recognize that the business they were in no longer exists. This applies not just to for-profit businesses, but to nonprofits, and even in certain important respects to churches."[2]

At the time the church world was contending with how to conduct and plan for the main event in the church calendar—Easter. Every playbook on how Easter service should run had to be thrown out the window. Every Western church was learning how to host a virtual service overnight, and its people and resources shifted to run a live-stream event. My church, *Ma Ke Alo o*, was no different; we felt the pressure of Easter Sunday and the loss of what could have been. The previous Easter Sunday, my church plant had hosted an evening conversation centered around Jesus at a trendy craft beer locale, where we hit our goal of having 50 percent non-Jesus-followers in the room. It was standing room only, with seventy people in attendance. It felt alive, fresh, and like it was hitting a mark. We planned to exceed one hundred people in 2020, and we were already celebrating. It would just be a matter of time before we would be looking for a new, larger location to host an even larger crowd of people.

In March of 2020, my church pivoted just like every church did. But instead of putting our people and resources into running a virtual Sunday service, we determined how we could honor our mission and the communities we served. We quickly surveyed the immediate needs in our local context and shifted our priorities to meet them.

We had invited some guests from a low-income senior living facility to attend our Easter gathering, and we heard that some of them had to get on a public bus to go to the food bank, pick up a can or two of nonperishables because that's all they could carry, and do this week in and week out. On Easter Sunday, we delivered a month's worth of groceries, donated from a variety of different organizations and individuals, to all seventy residents living in that facility.

We had invited some other seniors in another low-income building in our neighborhood to our Easter gathering, but instead, we dropped off a hot Easter dinner in partnership with a local restaurant that was asking for ways they could help the elderly. We provided a home-cooked dinner for over 250 grandmothers and grandfathers, none of whom could enjoy Easter dinner with their family that night.

We had invited a local community leader and her family to our Good Friday service to honor her efforts with the houseless population in Hawaii.

But we changed this plan as well. We had heard that her organization was being denied much-needed food donations because there was greater need elsewhere. On Easter Sunday, we partnered with a food bank to get enough boxes of canned and fresh foods to provide for every family in the community of three hundred she served in her neighborhood.

All of the friends, coworkers, family members, and neighbors we would have invited to our Easter service we instead invited to be a part of our response to those in need. It has continued like this ever since.

I was excited for one hundred people to come to an Easter service; God provided for nearly one thousand. That Easter I experienced what Jesus meant in his parable: "Still other seed fell on good soil, where it produced a crop—a hundred, sixty or thirty times what was sown" (Mt 13:8).

I think often about what made the difference. What was different about my church compared with other churches around me—not just in Hawaii, but across the Western church world? In my work as a local pastor and translocal network leader, I've had a front-row seat to observe the happenings of many churches across the board. Still, it wasn't immediately clear what made those in our church pivot so quickly to meet the needs of their neighbors. When the pandemic hit and the world seemed to unravel, we were only in the first two years of our communal life. What made the difference for our budding church?

Most people would speculate that it was because of our size—church plants are small, so it's easier for them to adapt and move in a different direction quickly. In 2019, prior to the pandemic, the US church was struggling. Close to three thousand Protestant churches launched in the United States that year, but approximately forty-five hundred shut down.[3] Daniel Im, coauthor of *Planting Missional Churches*, states, "While planting a church is still one of the most exciting things a pastor can do, over the past few years, I've noticed a growing hesitancy to plant, which is why these numbers don't surprise me."[4]

Church plants are not easy. And contrary to what some might think, the ability to pivot and move quickly in a different direction is not the norm in church-planting culture. Most churches, both established and newly planted, were responding to the pandemic in the same way—creating a digital platform. In a 2021 survey of 1,200 church leaders, 95 percent of leaders said their reliance on digital tools had increased compared with prior to the pandemic, nine out of ten churches used live-streaming as their main tool, and 51 percent reported launching this service during the pandemic.[5] A survey of over 550 churches found that "churches were willing to pivot quickly and change strategies when giving declined. But with rare exceptions, they tend to stick to their same ministry strategies that have led to declines in making new disciples."[6]

The difference in my church was not because it was a church plant. The difference in my church was discipleship.

In a church landscape where discipleship is at best at the periphery, my church centered discipleship from the beginning. We started, on purpose, with a small number of people (fifteen) called a "discipleship core" and met together twice a month to be purposefully equipped in the ways of Jesus. We defined discipleship as intentionally equipping people to imitate Jesus in his identity and praxis, and we kept this at the center of our church.

In a year's time, we journeyed together through five discipleship core essentials. We utilized a discipleship pathway, a framework for centering discipleship. At the same time we led a missional community, an identified space of mission in our neighborhood, where we could also practice living into the ways of Jesus. We hosted Open Spaces, a weekly community dinner where we "shared a meal and shared a story" regularly with thirty to fifty of our friends, neighbors, coworkers, and family members. Our aim for those community dinners was that 50 percent of the room would always be non-Jesus-followers. We also regularly became guests in the neighborhood by partnering with local organizations, businesses, and events on a monthly basis where we could share a practical experience to know and love the community we lived in.

For the first year, I never preached a sermon and my church never hosted a worship service. And although community and mission were happening, I did not lead the Open Spaces dinners nor the practical experiences. As the lead pastor of my church, I spent 90 percent of my time, effort, leadership, and resources on discipling those fifteen people. Ninety percent of my pastoral role was to develop a discipleship pathway and disciple my church through it. Ninety percent of my time was spent equipping disciples in order to multiply disciplemakers. The metric for leadership was not skill-based (teaching, preaching) or influence-based (ability to draw and command a crowd); the metric for leadership was in discipleship and disciple making.

Centering discipleship for my church produced something I was not prepared for. It generated maturity and multiplication.

The following year, after we finished our discipleship pathway together, we multiplied into three different missional communities. We went from one discipleship core leading one missional community into three discipleship cores each leading their own missional communities. We anticipate multiplying into nine different missional communities, serving over a thousand people, and discipling nearly a hundred imitators of Jesus.

Every disciple is discipled through a discipleship pathway with a group that journeys together. Every disciple in our church matures into the likeness of Christ within a community that is connected to mission. Each person imitates Jesus in their inner being (2 Cor 4:16), having the mind of Christ (1 Cor 2:16), navigating life with wisdom (1 Cor 1:30), and living into their sent-ness (Jn 20:21), both in their personal rhythms and within a gathered communal rhythm.

In March of 2020, when the world was faced with a pandemic that shut it down, the disciples in my church were more open and available to imitate Jesus. They had practiced living into this imitation for over a year now. They imitated him in their personal lives and imitated him in their communal lives. As imitators of Jesus, they were hopeful in the midst of discouragement and despair, actively pursued others, extended the sense of "family" in contrast to the world telling them to "protect their own," and showed self-giving love over selfishness more than anyone else in our culture and community. These disciples are now at the forefront, with other churches and organizations reaching out to them for expertise in how to meet community needs in Hawaii. They are seen as a pinnacle for how Christian community ought to be in our time.

PART 1

CHANGING OUR JOB DESCRIPTION

Ultimately, each church will be evaluated by only one thing—its disciples.

NEIL COLE

MAKING DISCIPLESHIP CENTRAL

Example is not the main thing. It is the only thing.

ALBERT SCHWEITZER

The LORD's eyes scan the whole world to find
those whose hearts are committed to him.

2 CHRONICLES 16:9 GW

I GREW UP IN WEST PHILADELPHIA. If you're from Philly, whether you're Black or White, Hispanic or Asian, blue-collar or white-collar, Muslim or Jew, during football season, you don green Eagles apparel whether or not you even know what football is. You practice your "fly eagle fly" dance, get your tailgating game on, and ready yourself for an intense season of Sunday night football viewing. Every. Sunday. Night.

I also happen to be a doctor, and on one particular Sunday night, I had an ER shift. Everyone who has been in the emergency room knows the chaos that exists in that high-volume, high-risk, high-intensity environment. Quick triaging and transporting of patients to makeshift hospital beds, assessing life-and-death situations at every turn, dealing with screaming babies with high fevers, assessing gunshot wounds and abdominal lacerations, managing acute heart attacks and stroke cases, and cleaning up buckets of vomiting. When you go into your ER shift, you know to expect categorized chaos. But if you live in Philadelphia, and you're wearing your green Eagles apparel, and it's a Sunday night when your favorite football team is playing, even in the emergency room it's dead silent.

It was one of those Sunday nights for me. In a room with an occupancy of fifty patients, we had three people on gurneys. There was such a lull that we pulled all the individual curtains back, turned all the TVs to face the central nursing station, and all of us—doctors, nurses, janitors, and medical technicians—watched the Eagles game from wherever we were.

Like clockwork, as soon as that three-hour game was over, it was like someone pushed a button. Anyone experiencing medical discomfort in their body suddenly decided to proceed to the nearest emergency room. The moment the game was over, patients started pouring in. It was a wonder that cardiac arrests could arrest themselves until a Sunday night Eagles game was over.

In a city like that, being a fan was not an option—it was a mandate. But over the years I began to be able to tell the fans from the followers. The bandwagoners versus the diehards. Those who paid attention only when the Eagles had a chance at the Super Bowl and those who supported the team even when they probably wouldn't make the playoffs. Mere fans versus true followers. Fans just join in the fun; followers support, rally, and carry their team through the thickest of seasons.

This isn't just true in sports either. A superficiality of fanhood is emerging throughout contemporary culture via social media. Communications professor Brandi Watkins notes that, among social media influencers (SMIs), "the lengths someone will go to in order to maintain their status as an influencer are astonishing, as are the many pitfalls that are associated with the pressures of being an SMI."[1] The social media culture has become a race to see who has the most followers and to try desperately to appease them, with threat of being "unfollowed" ever present. Influencers know that followers and fans are one and the same. There is less and less distinguishing mere fans from true followers.

MERE FANS VERSUS TRUE FOLLOWERS

Second Chronicles 14–16 highlights the reign of Judah's king Asa, whose "heart was fully committed to the LORD all his life" (2 Chron 15:17). Yet after gaining safety for Judah against surrounding nations by relying on God, in the thirty-sixth year of his reign Asa makes an unwise treaty with the king of Aram, using silver and gold from the Lord's temple to maintain his own security at the expense of Israel's. Hanani the seer goes to the king and says:

> Were not the Cushites and Libyans a mighty army with great numbers of chariots and horsemen? Yet when you relied on the LORD, he delivered them into your hand. For the eyes of the LORD range throughout the earth to strengthen those whose hearts are fully committed to him. You have done a foolish thing, and from now on you will be at war. (2 Chron 16:8-9)

God is not looking for mere fans; he's searching for true followers, those whose hearts are fully committed to him. He's not looking for band-wagoners who cheer him on in easier seasons, nor is he concerned with our fair-weather decisions on following or unfollowing him. God is looking for true followers who rely on him, follow him, rest in him, and are renewed by him. Being a true follower means being a disciple, and discipleship is important to God. In all four of the Gospel accounts, from the very beginning Jesus calls ordinary people to follow him.[2] In the New Testament, "following" and "discipleship" are synonymous because they're translated from the same Greek word, *mathētēs*. As such, Matthew 16:24 can be translated several ways:

> Whoever wants to be my disciple must deny themselves and take up their cross and follow me. (NIV)

> If anyone would come after me, let him deny himself and take up his cross and follow me. (ESV)

> If any of you wants to be my follower, you must give up your own way, take up your cross, and follow me. (NLT)

The word *mathētēs* refers to a learner, apprentice, pupil, adherent, or follower.[3] The apostle Paul and other New Testament writers further define being a follower and disciple of Jesus by using the word *mimētēs*,[4] which translates as "imitating" and is where the English word "mimic" comes from. Thus 1 Corinthians 11:1 can be translated as:

Follow my example, as I follow the example of Christ. (NIV)

Be imitators of me, as I am of Christ. (NRSV)

Be ye followers of me, even as I also am of Christ. (KJV)

Therefore, when we look at the entirety of the New Testament and its references to being a follower and a disciple, it's safe to conclude that to the first-century Christians, being a follower of Jesus was about imitating Jesus.

Fans will often say, "I think I really like you, and I like what you stand for in certain areas, and I think I can identify with this as long as we're in a good season." But Jesus isn't looking for fans; he's searching for followers—people who will follow him no matter what, whose hearts are fully committed to him. People who say, "No matter the circumstance, whatever the season, I'm with you, Jesus. Wherever you want to go, whatever you want to do, I am with you no matter what. I'm going to follow you in all respects and I identify with and choose you above all other things." Jesus also isn't looking for just one person; he's searching to and fro for a community of people whose hearts are for one another because their hearts are fully committed to him. People who move into neighborhoods and create networks of culture and community around them to follow Jesus into all the nooks and crannies where the Holy Spirit is already at work (Jn 13:35).

Discipleship—being a true follower of God and imitating Jesus—is what God himself is using to transform and redeem the whole world. A sending (missional) and trinitarian (communal) God is transforming and redeeming the world through true followers who imitate him in both his missional and communal nature. Discipleship is central to this.

Are you a disciple of Jesus? Is your community a community of disciples of Jesus?

THE MAIN THING

In Matthew 28, Jesus gives a final address to his disciples:

All authority in heaven and on earth has been given to me. Therefore go and make disciples of all nations, baptizing them in the name of the Father and of the Son and of the Holy Spirit, and teaching them to obey everything I have commanded you. And surely I am with you always, to the very end of the age. (Mt 28:18-20)

As with most subtitled movies, we don't really understand the heart of what's going on unless we go back to the original language. A common misnomer about this passage is that Jesus is giving us a list of suggested tasks; we pick a couple and we're good to go. But Jesus isn't giving us options. This is not a top ten list of recommendations for living a good life. In the original Greek, Jesus is commanding his disciples to do just one thing: make disciples.

Murray Harris notes in *Navigating Tough Texts* that the word translated "go" is often misunderstood as a command, when in actuality it's a participle—"going"—that highlights the main command.[5] In other words, Jesus is saying to his followers, "I have all the power and authority you'll ever need. In light of that, I'm assuming you'll go out. As you go out, there's one main thing I want you to focus on: make disciples. Doing this one thing brings others into a journey of becoming committed to the communal and sending God. And don't forget, I am with you wherever you go, even to the very end."

If discipleship is the main thing and it means imitating Jesus, then we as leaders ought to consider the following questions:

- Am I a disciple of Jesus? How do I know I'm a disciple of Jesus?

- Do I make disciples? Have I ever discipled someone else?

If Jesus says being a disciple and making disciples is the main thing, then that's the main thing for us. But what in the world does this look like? How do we know for certain that this is happening in our own life? What is present in our life that makes us say, "I am a disciple"? Or, "That girl is a disciple for sure!"

Most people answer this question in the theoretical: "A disciple is someone who lives a surrendered life." Or, "A disciple is someone who's in love with Jesus." While these are good things to be, they aren't tangible enough to properly answer the question. Which leaves us at the same place we started. How do we know that a person is living a surrendered life? How do people actually show that they're in love with Jesus?

We as leaders understand the sentiment behind being disciples and the good intentions that go along with it, but we don't always know exactly what we're looking for or need to focus on. And if I don't know how to tangibly identify a disciple, then realistically, I don't know how to go about making one. Speaking from my own experience, I knew how to escort people into Christian culture. I knew how to help people come to church, join a small group, and get involved in serving the church. Was this how to make a *disciple*? I could teach people to learn how to read the Bible and pray, but was this how to *make* a disciple? Since I participated in these activities myself, did this make *me* a disciple of Jesus?

Something didn't sit right with me; there had to be more. And I knew there had to be more because the people I read about who were called Jesus' disciples were not living the kind of life I saw the people who called themselves disciples living in the church today. Jesus said he came so we would have life and have it abundantly (Jn 10:10), but when I looked around, it seemed like that abundant life was alluded to—like a dream or wishful thinking—but never really lived out.

DISCIPLESHIP AS PERIPHERAL

Somehow along the way, discipleship became synonymous with assimilation into church culture. Making disciples came to mean helping people participate in Christian activities. While being a disciple of Jesus involves partnering with the local church, it is by no means the full picture. If we honestly and humbly examine ourselves and our leadership, we must admit to living in self-deception: making disciples has become the same thing as making a worship service gathering or, at its extreme, a megachurch.

Sociologists Wellman, Corcoran, and Stockly-Meyerdirk state, "The megachurches movement is one of the leading indicators of how American Christians exercise their faith these days. . . . Megachurch services feature a come-as-you-are atmosphere, rock music and a multisensory mélange of visuals and other elements to stimulate the senses, as well as small group participation and a shared focus on the message from a charismatic pastor."[6] Practical metrics of church attendance and financial prosperity are the two fruit we look for in evaluating whether we've made disciples. We have perpetuated a culture of spectators and nonparticipants that bears no fruit. We at best cultivate a weekly variety show that highlights a TED-like talk bookended by a local unpaid band, often paying for either smoke machines or organ maintenance. This ritual actually pushes discipleship more and more into the margins while tethering people more firmly to consumerism. Our stage productions depend financially and culturally on spectatorship.

I am not satisfied with this. I don't think you're satisfied with this either. I don't think you're satisfied with the people we lead and love investing their efforts in a weekly stage production rather than the needs of their neighborhoods and communities. I don't think you're satisfied with our congregants being "discipled" by sermons or musical experiences instead of being intentionally equipped. I want God's people to get up out of the seats and fully participate in the abundant life Jesus offers all of us. I want them to experience the fruit that all of us are called to bear. I want them to bear that fruit for the sake of their neighbors, coworkers, families, and friends.

DISCIPLESHIP AS CENTRAL

A custom in our household is that when you become a teenager, you trek the steep terrain to conquer the first of three peaks of Mount Olomana, the iconic giant overshadowing the windward side of Oahu. Every year after that, you traverse that mountain peak by peak until you're able to reach the ultimate summit. Our sixteen- and fifteen-year-old have summited this mountain with my husband using all the bouldering techniques and ropes required; our youngest will begin her trek next year. Steve and I initiated this tradition for our children not because it has anything to do with climbing but because it has everything to do with discipleship.

Climbing Mount Olomana is intended for our children to experience the journey firsthand, recognizing its importance, hardship, and beauty and being guided compassionately and patiently by someone who's just a little further ahead. By revisiting the same mountain year in and year out, they notice their own growth and progress, discovering that the ropes segment they once found terrifying is now less so, the grip that took forever to learn is now a breeze, and the climb that once produced uncertainty and hesitation now yields pleasure and expectation. Climbing Mount Olomana each year is akin to a discipleship pathway for our teenage children, and in our family we keep discipleship central. More than anything else, we strive to equip our children to leave our home for the adventure that awaits them as they mature and flourish in the way of Jesus for the sake of those around them.

Likewise, our local church community keeps discipleship central by orienting our life around it. Every owner (member) of our church community is discipled along a discipleship pathway in the context of a community that's tethered to a place (neighborhood) or space (network) of mission for renewal. Every owner revisits the discipleship pathway year by year within a community. Every disciple experiences discipleship firsthand, recognizing its importance, hardship, and beauty, and is led by folks who are just a little further ahead of them in the journey. While the trek may differ from time to time (perhaps experiencing a change in weather, terrain, guide, or individual experience), we all follow the same discipleship pathway.

Following the same discipleship pathway allows the community to notice our own growth and progress, and the familiarity of the journey produces joy and expectation. We not only see more and more ways we are individually and communally imitating Jesus, but we imitate his compassion and patience to journey alongside others in their discipleship. By moving discipleship from the periphery to the center, we are able to definitively say, "I am a disciple of Jesus, I know how I am a disciple of Jesus, and I know how to make disciples of Jesus."

If we're honest with ourselves, many of the places of Christian worship we attend have an underlying assumption that if we just maintain a weekly Sunday gathering where we hope and pray for an increased number of attendees, a thirty-minute oration and thirty minutes of singing religious songs will make disciples who live as a community for the sake of the world and culture around them. At best, discipleship becomes additive: an attendee feels a spark of inspiration from a message or song and invites her coworker the following week, hoping and praying that a thirty-minute oration and thirty minutes of singing religious songs will make her co-worker into an imitator of Jesus. Even the most ideal version of this adds to a growing mindset of spectatorship where we simply gather weekly to listen to a speaker and hear musicians.

The praxis of imitating Christ has nothing to do with just listening and hearing. Jesus closes his Sermon on the Mount, where he offers practical wisdom about how to live like him for the sake of the culture and world around us, with this:

> Likewise, every good tree bears good fruit, but a bad tree bears bad fruit. A good tree cannot bear bad fruit, and a bad tree cannot bear good fruit. Every tree that does not bear good fruit is cut down and thrown into the fire. Thus, by their fruit you will recognize them.
>
> Not everyone who says to me, "Lord, Lord," will enter the kingdom of heaven, but only the one who does the will of my Father who is in heaven. Many will say to me on that day, "Lord, Lord, did we not prophesy in your name and in your name drive out demons and in your name perform many miracles?" Then I will tell them plainly, "I never knew you. Away from me, you evildoers!"
>
> Therefore everyone who hears these words of mine and puts them into practice is like a wise man who built his house on the rock. The rain came down, the streams rose, and the winds blew and beat against that house; yet it did not fall, because it had its foundation on the rock. But everyone who hears these words of mine and does not put them into practice is like a foolish man who built his house on sand. The rain came down, the streams rose, and the winds blew and beat against that house, and it fell with a great crash. (Mt 7:17-27)

Jesus is saying that Christlike praxis is about listening and doing. Christlike praxis is about seeing the fruit of transformation and renewal not only in his disciples but through his disciples. A sent community of people who listens to Jesus and does what he tells them to do together will not be limited to gathering weekly to listen to a sermon and sing songs. They'll be on the move together into the culture and world around them. Living into the praxis of self-giving love as a sent community is not an elective for disciples of Jesus. It's the main thing.

A NOTE ON SUNDAY SERVICES

It's worth mentioning that as we immerse ourselves in the work of moving discipleship from the periphery to the center, it will often feel at odds with our current framework in how to "do church," most specifically in how we view our weekly Sunday worship services. I am in no way trying to minimize the importance, history, and value of the community congregating as a response in public worship and celebration of God; on the contrary, I am delineating the difference between intentional discipleship and equipping and intentional worship and proclamation. They are not interchangeable. The crowds in the Gospel accounts were often astounded by what Jesus did, but few remained behind to be his true followers.[7] In keeping discipleship central, we as leaders also need to view our public worship services appropriately, neither heralding them as the main measure of success nor minimizing them into privatized and individualized religion. JR Woodward writes:

> We need to move from idolizing or demonizing public [worship] space, to re-imagining it for our context today. We need to develop a theology of the crowds which prevents us from insidiously becoming captive to them or allured by them, to finding ways to spontaneously and subversively proclaim the Good News in a way that unmasks the ideologies that people are captive to, and opens their eyes to the reality of the kingdom of God.[8]

While moving discipleship from periphery to center can and ought to coincide with a compelling public worship that proclaims the reality of the kingdom of God, centering discipleship emphasizes that imitating Jesus doesn't mainly happen in public worship.

IMITATION GAME

When we as leaders make the pointed decision to move discipleship from periphery to center, we are making a hopeful and calculated decision to embed discipleship within a reimagined framework. We're stating that imitation is more important than instruction. We want disciples doing life amid a missional (sent) community that's a vibrant part of the local context rather than an institutionalized and overgeneralized (and non-decolonized) church. We see a vision for the movement of the kingdom of God on this side of new creation over paltry social clubs and charity events. When we begin the good and hard work of making discipleship central, we dedicate our own leadership to imitation, communities on mission together, and a vision for movement.

Table 1.1. Leadership focus: Centered versus peripheral discipleship

Leadership	Centered discipleship	Peripheral discipleship
Emphasis on:	Imitation (discipleship)	Instruction (sermon)
Moving people to:	Community around them	Sunday worship service
Vision for:	Movement	Church

The apostle Paul invites the churches in Corinth to imitate him as he imitates Christ (1 Cor 11:1 GW). But in our local community, I am not the person the community is trying to imitate. The community actually imitates Melissa as she imitates Christ. An office manager and mother of two, Melissa took on the role of organizing a weekly potluck community dinner from year one and improved it leaps and bounds by setting it up in her own condominium. She strategically counted how many households were within her "neighborhood," invited them to pull up a beach chair or dining chair right outside their front doors, and led them in talking story together in a regular rhythm. As the disciples within that neighborhood committed themselves to pray for their immediate next-door neighbors, this simple dinner grew into a force to be reckoned with. That lower-middle-class former farming community is now a spearhead in meeting the needs of the impoverished around them.

The community imitates Timmy as he imitates Christ. Timmy is a physical therapist and was once a self-proclaimed come-late-leave-early church attendee. He committed himself to a discipleship core to be more fully equipped and is now leading, teaching, and equipping a new group of disciples, intentionally helping them partner with organizations like the Boys and Girls Clubs and the local food bank to connect Christlike identity to Christlike praxis.

The community imitates Keven as he imitates Christ. A former tennis all-star, Keven combined his passion for sports with Jesus' heart for his community. He started a missional community oriented around pickleball and is now intentionally connecting that community to discipleship, where non-Jesus-followers are attending a worship service for the first time.

The community imitates Kelci, a hospice nurse and impassioned advocate for the elderly who invites others to care for the low-income seniors in her neighborhood (all five hundred of them, who know her by name). She has discipled them in such a manner that these disciples are now discipling the seniors they faithfully love and serve—they've learned the secret of not just doing meaningful charitable work but connecting it the centrality of discipleship.

I invite you to consider holding both your perception and perspective on discipleship with open hands. I invite you to consider hitting the pause button on your regular ways of regarding discipleship. I invite you to step back and see a bigger, wider vision for discipleship as central. This book is intended to lead you out of the weeds and into centered, practical discipleship that transforms our communities. This requires assessing both our traditional interpretations of discipleship and our point of view on its role in our lives. I invite you to make discipleship central.

2

THE NATURE OF DISCIPLESHIP

Imitation is not just the sincerest form of flattery;
it's the sincerest form of learning.

GEORGE BERNARD SHAW

Imitate me as I imitate Christ.

1 CORINTHIANS 11:1 GW

MY SON BEREN LOVES BASEBALL. He's been playing since he was four years old. He absolutely devours this game and every inch of culture that revolves around it, from the lineups to the ERAs to the philosophy of managing a major league team. During the season, he'll regale us daily with stats from his beloved Phillies, and in the summer, when baseball is not in season, he informs us of all the possible trades happening. He spent hours on the field practicing with his Little League team, and now, as a near-adult who joins any league he can get into, he spends hours at home practicing his pitches. The first thing he talks about when he wakes up is how he thinks his team is going to do today, the first thing he tells me when he comes home from school is how his team actually did, and the last thing he tells me before going to bed is how he thinks his team will do tomorrow. One summer my husband took him to a baseball clinic with the acclaimed Tom House (throw-mechanics guru to the likes of Tom Brady and Nolan Ryan), and Beren went every day for an entire week, for hours. He threw and threw and batted and batted. For hours.

The thing is, Beren doesn't love baseball, study everything about it, and eagerly anticipate the next game win or lose because he went to the elite Tom House training program. Beren loves baseball because he takes after his dad. And Steve is not the kind of dad who drives his kids hard in sports. On the contrary, he's gentle and kind and wins coach of the year every year because of how he treats his players. He esteems character over skill, growth over winning. Beren loves baseball because Steve loves baseball; Beren plays baseball because he imitates his dad.

Discipleship is no different. Meli disciples Monica because she imitates me as I imitate Christ. Meli is a petite Asian woman, highly intellectual, an attorney who graduated from one of the top law schools in the nation. She could have had her choice of legal firm to work for but decided on a public-interest nonprofit organization. That's where she met Monica, a fellow lover of advocacy. Meli started a weekly lunch prayer gathering at her workplace, open to both Jesus-followers and non-, and started discipling Monica through a discipleship pathway. How did Meli know to do this? Because she had been through a discipleship pathway with another group of people, one where we journeyed together learning about things such as how to articulate the full gospel and what it looks like to have a heart for the one, just as Jesus proclaimed the good news and sought after the one. Discipleship is about imitation.

NOT A PROGRAM

If discipleship is about imitation, then discipleship is not a program. Discipleship can't be a program. When Jesus called every one of his followers to make disciples, he wasn't calling us to a systematic program; he was calling us to a new way of life.

> Then he called the crowd to him along with his disciples and said: "Whoever wants to be my disciple must deny themselves and take up their cross and follow me. For whoever wants to save their life will lose it, but whoever loses their life for me and for the gospel will save it." (Mk 8:34-35)

If you're looking for a fancy discipleship program to implement into your church structure, this is not for you. Now, I'm not against programs;

in fact, I've been through world-class training programs to hone a variety of skills in my life, but discipleship just doesn't work that way. Discipleship is a way of living. And a program that works for one person doesn't necessarily work for someone else. Remember, the aim is not to provide a one-size-fits-all, step-by-step methodology that is guaranteed to help you change your life. Honestly, we are too unique and complicated a people to have a one-size-fits-all program.

According to the Merriam-Webster Dictionary, a program is an "outline of the order to be followed, of the features to be presented, and the person participating; a plan or system under which action may be taken toward a goal." The Collins Dictionary defines it as "a plan of action to accomplish a specified end." In contrast, "framework" is defined in the Oxford Learner's Dictionary as "a basic structure underlying a system, concept or text." In other words, a framework is a "conceptual structure intended to serve as a support or guide for the building of something that expands the structure into something useful."[1]

A discipleship pathway is not a discipleship program. A discipleship pathway is a framework for your church to center discipleship. It's a way to guide your community and build infrastructure to help them expand discipleship beyond the framework. While a program such as Alcoholics Anonymous intends for people to follow its specific steps and protocols to accomplish a goal together, a framework uses a conceptual structure to place helpful guideposts that show which direction to go. While a program will utilize one route and order to get to a goal, a framework allows flexibility for an assortment of routes and orders to get to a goal. A program is seldom altered; a framework allows for adaptability and versatility. A program banks on the content; a framework looks at what's being produced.

A discipleship pathway allows flexibility and a variety of tools for people to become disciples of Jesus.

TWO DISCIPLESHIP QUESTIONS

With that being said, in order to be disciples of Jesus, we need to be able to answer two specific questions:

- How do I know I'm a disciple of Jesus?

- Do I know how to make disciples of Jesus?

One of the biggest misnomers about discipleship is that only the "special" or "chosen ones" have the ability and prowess to disciple others, but this couldn't be further from the truth. Every single Christian, every person who follows Jesus, is able not only to be a disciple but to disciple others. And all of us have these abilities because of the Holy Spirit residing inside us. Philippians 1:6 reminds us that the God who started a good work in every one of us will make sure it gets completed. It isn't a matter of *if* you'll grow to be able to disciple others; it's a matter of *how* you'll grow to disciple others. My hope is that understanding this will help you grow in not only being a disciple yourself but also in going and making disciples of other people.

So, let's start by asking that question: What does discipleship look like? Or, put differently, how would you complete this statement?

"I know I've been discipled because _____."

Most of us think we're disciples because we go to church regularly, live a decently moral life, have been baptized, and have perhaps attended a discipleship class. Our internal checkmarks on this list reassure us, and in turn we run others through this same list to assure them they have been discipled. But church attendance, a label of not being "bad," baptism, and Sunday school participation are not merely what Jesus meant when he called us to be and make disciples. None of these assurances mark us as people who are actively imitating Jesus and intentionally following him.

What it does do is give us a false narrative for what it means to be a disciple of Christ. We think listening to a weekly sermon, abstaining from a list of immoral acts such as murder and adultery, at some point making a private decision to be baptized (whether our parents made it for us or not), and taking a bonus class at church give us a golden ticket to heaven. Discipleship is not about a free pass to heaven or a false retirement as we wait patiently for our time to come.

Discipleship—being a disciple and making disciples—is about becoming more like Christ, taking on both his identity and his praxis. Denying ourselves, taking up our cross daily, and following him (Lk 9:23) means taking on his identity and mission of self-giving love, identified as participating in a sent community of people on mission together. Lesslie Newbigin writes:

> The task of ministry is to lead the congregation as a whole in a mission to the community as a whole, to claim its whole public life, as well as the personal lives of all its people, for God's rule. It means equipping all the members of the congregation to understand and fulfill their several roles in this mission through their faithfulness in their daily work. It means training and equipping them to be active followers of Jesus in his assault on the principalities and powers which he has disarmed on his cross. And it means sustaining them in bearing the cost of that warfare.[2]

David Bosch furthers this point when he states, "Mission has its origin in the heart of God. God is a fountain of sending love. This is the deepest source of mission. It is impossible to penetrate deeper still; there is mission because God loves people."[3]

Table 2.1. Misleading marks of discipleship

What we do	What we think
Go to church regularly	Many Christians believe attending a Sunday service marks them as disciples of Jesus. Many Christian leaders believe having people listen to a Sunday sermon is what disciples them. This notion is the same as when people join a gym, particularly after the holiday season. You're not fit just because you bought a membership to the gym, and simply walking into the gym doesn't get you in shape. In the same way, attending church regularly on Sunday mornings doesn't warrant us to be fit to be disciples.
Live a moral life	Many Christians believe being a "good" or moral person, doing moral things, and living a moral life is the definition of being a follower of Jesus, but it actually couldn't be further from the truth. Jesus isn't just about morality, being a model citizen, philanthropy, or living by a set of rules, and none of these things themselves show us to be his disciples.
Undergo baptism	Instead of experiencing the beauty and power of baptism to transform us into a new person and disciple of Jesus, we cheapen and minimize it by participating in baptism without pairing it with deep equipping to become disciples of Jesus. Essentially, this is the same thing as a couple saying that just because they participated in a wedding ceremony, they can now sit back and not participate in daily married life.

Table 2.1. (continued)

What we do	What we think
Attend a class on discipleship 	All business executives know the falsehood that earning an MBA straight out of college makes young people great business practitioners because they went through an in-depth learning process. Being knowledgeable is not the same thing as being experienced, and this is no different when it comes to learning about discipleship versus living discipleship out.

The fact remains that, while all of these things are good things, they don't necessarily mean you've been discipled. They probably fall into the category of good examples of tools for discipleship than measures of discipleship itself. The measure of discipleship is the kind of fruit a disciple produces. While tools point to a certain method, fruit points to what a disciple is deeply rooted and growing in. What fruit are you looking for that marks a disciple of Jesus?

LOOK FOR FRUIT

What do I mean by this? Let's say your job is to turn a young sapling into a tree that bears fruit. You do some research and even ask an arborist about the best way to attain your goal, and you're provided with a variety of methods to tend to this young sapling: use a fertilizer specific to its needs, place it in a greenhouse at such-and-such stage to optimize its growth, and water it in a specific pattern and time of day. While all of these methods are important and helpful in nurturing this sapling into a fruit-bearing tree, you would never think you'd accomplished your goal just because you put that sapling in a greenhouse. Box checked. Or because you watered it in a particular way today. Job well done. No. You would not measure getting the job done by the methods used; instead, you would look at the sapling itself and see if it was growing into a tree that bears fruit.

In caring for a tree, we would not equate the tools with the actual fruit. The measure of a tool's effectiveness would simply be this: does the tree bear fruit?

The same is true for discipleship. The aim is to see people grow and produce kingdom fruit. Christine Pohl writes, "The best testimony to the truth of the gospel is the quality of our life together. Jesus risked his reputation and the credibility of his story by tying them to how his followers live and care for one another in community."[4] Producing kingdom fruit looks like an identity rooted in becoming more like Christ, committed to a sent community of people who are demonstrating Jesus' love, and being on mission together for the sake of the world.

Yet we live in a day and age where the means and the methods have become confused with the end. We often equate a person's growth with the tool they used. If a person has taken a class on discipleship, we count them as discipled. If someone has acquired a wealth of scriptural knowledge, we assume they have a personal relationship with God. If someone has made a private decision about their faith, we move on to the next person to be baptized. Again, while these methods may assist in the process of discipleship, they are not indicators of discipleship.

The only way to know for sure that people are growing and being discipled as followers of Jesus is to look for fruit.

DISCIPLESHIP PATHWAY

A discipleship pathway helps us clearly live in a way that's connected to Jesus and bears fruit in the way of Jesus. A discipleship pathway is a resource that helps us know if a person is growing and being discipled as a follower of Jesus and bearing fruit. A discipleship pathway is also experienced by a closed group of people, a bounded set that I call a discipleship core. A discipleship pathway is best utilized in a discipleship core that is tethered to a community of people who are on mission together, that is, they are actively seeking the renewal of the community and culture around them together.

Table 2.2. Discipleship connected to community and mission

Formation	People	Renewal
Resource	Community	Mission
Discipleship pathway	Discipleship core	Neighborhood/network

Developing a discipleship pathway has the clear goal of intentionally multiplying disciples over Sunday spectators. Constructing one is not about establishing another program; it is a means of praxis geared toward helping disciples experience and bear conclusive kingdom fruit in their lives and the lives of others. The goal of constructing a clear discipleship pathway is not to implement another teaching; rather, the goal of using a discipleship pathway—to be and make disciples of Jesus—is to mature in the identity and purpose of Christ. Neil Cole writes:

> Ultimately, each church will be evaluated by only one thing—its disciples. Your church is only as good as her disciples. It does not matter how good your praise, preaching, programs or property are; if your disciples are passive, needy, consumeristic, and not [moving in the direction of radical obedience,] your church is not good.[5]

In Jesus' own words, he's out to reform and transform us to be his disciples, people who don't live passive, needy, consumeristic lives but lives that imitate his. This undoubtedly means that if we make discipleship the center of what we do, then our churches and communities will become people of radical love and radical obedience, living wholeheartedly and intentionally to be sent into the world for the sake of the world. But if we forsake our most basic task of making disciples, then our churches and communities will be limited and its people likewise. We must ask ourselves the same question that Dallas Willard asked: "What is our plan for discipleship? Is our plan working?"[6]

HEART BEHIND DISCIPLESHIP

In the Gospel of Mark, Jesus and his disciples are traveling through a city called Caesarea Philippi, a place where people from all over the world were known to sit around and talk about spiritual things. So while crowds of people gather around and talk about who their gods are, Jesus asks his disciples, "Who do people say that I am?" They reply, "Some say that you're [this or that prophet of old]" (Mark 8:27-29).

My husband and I traveled that same trek when we visited Israel a few years back, and we saw that the striking scene when Jesus asked his question was against the backdrop of a mountainside carved with inlets of various sizes to house the physical idols of that time. It was a destination for claiming who or what you worshiped. It was in this cultural setting that Jesus asked his disciples, "Who do *you* say that I am?"

This pivotal moment revealed the manner in which the disciples themselves were connecting to Jesus. This is ultimately the heart behind discipleship. It's to pour into a person in order for them to be able to answer, "Who do *you* say that Jesus is?" It's to connect to him and walk in community throughout your life out of that personal relationship with Jesus.

Those of us who have been around church culture for a while probably get a specific image when I say the word "discipleship." For some of us, we were exposed to a program, Bible study, or training of some sort: a Sunday school seminar, Wednesday evening church special, or weekly small group. For others, we think that it's equivalent to something like mentorship or "doing life together." While discipleship may contain elements of these things, it's not primarily these things.

WHAT DISCIPLESHIP IS NOT

I define discipleship by describing what it is *not*. The primary disguises of discipleship are: supervision, friendship, counseling, and training. As we go through each, we'll constantly go back to the heart behind discipleship.

Table 2.3. Disguises of discipleship

Type	Characteristic
Supervision	Structure > Relationship
Friendship	Structure < Relationship
Counseling	Inward-focused > Outward-focused
Training	Inward-focused < Outward-focused

Not just supervision. The role of a supervisor is primarily to provide structure and goals for the sake of the company or task at hand. While this may involve a level of apprenticeship and training, the interaction is based solely on accomplishing a goal. There's no real need for a semblance of personal relationship. The supervisee's position could be terminated at any moment based on their performance on the job. Discipleship is *not* a contract between the supervisor and the supervised, where the arranged structure drives the majority of the relationship and purpose.

Not just friendship. Friendship in our day and age contrasts starkly with how Jesus defines friendship. Jesus wants to transform his friends through intentional discipleship. He wants to disciple people through profound friendship. In our culture, friendship is often built around common interests and compatible personalities without a common purpose; it thrives more on an "organic" schedule over structure, often with little space for intentionally challenging one another toward growth. Friendship today wants to maintain the relationship at all cost without challenging or sharpening one another nor striving toward a common goal. While relationship is of great importance, it isn't the highest purpose for discipleship. Discipleship is *not* a bond between friends, where today's culture defines friendship as being organic, unstructured, and comfortable.

Not just counseling. The counselor's role for the counselee is fundamentally to give advice to help the individual in their personal challenges and growth. Counseling often is arranged by the counselee, who sets the terms for their inner emotional needs while the counselor provides services to help them toward emotional health. While this is helpful to a person in seasons of need, the focus is on the individual and only the individual's needs. Discipleship is *not* about moving inward toward individual emotional health where the entire topic of discussion is about the person being poured into and that person alone.

Not just training. The goal of the trainer is to instill in the trainee a set of specific skills in order to accomplish a specific task. It has nothing to do with relationship nor with the trainee's inner person. While some could develop character while learning these set skills, such as professional athletes or military personnel, most people who receive some sort of on-the-job training acquire a certain skill to be able to do a certain job. Discipleship is *not* about being driven and equipped to only perform a task or accomplish a goal.

What, then, is discipleship?

Discipleship is clearly and intentionally abiding in God and living in his kingdom reality and helping others abide in God and live in his kingdom reality.

It's about following and imitating Jesus *and* helping others follow and imitate Jesus. It's meant for everyone and not just some. It's meant to imitate Jesus and to have concrete models around us in order to imitate Jesus. Discipleship is about being inward-focused so that our inner person will be transformed into the likeness of Jesus *and* outward-focused in how we allow Jesus to shape how we live our lives. It's about being formed and forming others for the sake of mission and sentness. It's about having an active personal connection to Jesus and leading others to have active personal connections to Jesus that produce an abundant life and the flourishing of the world around us.

A WORD ON DISQUALIFICATION

A brief note on self-disqualification. Don't do it. Don't buy into it. In following Jesus, discipleship is not optional nor only for elite Christians. It's not meant to be a complicated practice nor a set of accomplishments to be checked off; it's not a performance-driven test.

It's meant to be a way of life.

Some of us may think things like, *I'd love to participate in discipleship, but, honestly, I don't have time. I don't really have the skill set to do it. I don't really have the knowledge base to do it. I don't even know what to do. I'm not really likable enough to do it.* While it's natural for these fears and concerns to come up, they're not meant to be our norm. They're not meant to have the final say about us.

Jesus calls *all* of us to go and make disciples.

DISCIPLESHIP HAPPENS IN COMMUNITY

Here's where a discipleship pathway is vital. It brings clarity to the basic essentials to grow more in the maturity and likeness of Jesus. Because the essentials for maturity are clear, the tools to develop it in people are numerous. A discipleship pathway can be used in a variety of ways by a variety of people, and it happens alongside a committed community of people. Discipleship happens best in community, and community happens best on mission together.

Mission cannot be teased apart from local community just as discipleship cannot truly happen outside of a community. Phil Meadows, professor of disciple making and missional ecclesiology, writes:

> If we first seek to make disciples, we will become vital congregations, have authentic worship, experience real fellowship and develop effective mission. But, if we start with a mission strategy, we usually end up running programs rather than sharing faith. If we start with community, we may end up with social circles rather than spiritual communities. If we start with church service, we are likely to end up as consumers rather than disciples.[7]

I will go one step further. If we first seek to make disciples who are on mission together within a thriving, liberating, welcoming, healing, and learning community, we will become a vital movement. We will have authentic experiences of the power and beauty of Jesus, who deserves our whole-life worship. We will experience and provide a real sense of belonging and purpose, and develop effective mission for the sake of the world around us—for the sake of our families, friends, coworkers, and neighbors.

This is what discipleship at the center of community looks like.

3

THE MARKS OF A MATURE DISCIPLE

*There is no participation in Christ without
participation in his mission to the world.*

KARL BARTH

*Whoever wants to be my disciple must deny themselves and
take up their cross and follow me. For whoever wants to save
their life will lose it, but whoever loses their life for me will find it.*

MATTHEW 16:24-25

I HAVE DEGREES IN BOTH AFRICAN STUDIES and neuroscience, which means I am fluent in Kiswahili and can tell you how neurotransmitters work. Despite having a bilingual background, I was not prepared for how different Swahili was, and it took me a while to feel comfortable with the Bantu language. The grammar felt different from both English and Korean, and some of the unique sounds were foreign to my tongue; I sounded like an infant East African. Despite memorizing sentence structures and vocabulary, as soon as I opened my mouth, I did not sound like I spoke Swahili.

It wasn't until I lived in a Swahili-speaking country that I began to mature in learning and speaking the language. I was fortunate enough to do a Fulbright in Tanzania, and I was immersed in the language day in and day out. My Tanzanian peers and instructors, while humored by my infancy, were warm and encouraging as they helped me grow in my language learning. The rigor of a Fulbright scholarship entails research, and I had chosen the topic of women's health in Morogoro, Tanzania, a small rural setting where most women thought malaria was the same thing as the flu and was transmitted by dust. I worked at a women's health clinic where a Pakistani English-speaking physician was the director. Because I was growing in my fluency, I was brought on to translate for the physician and patients. By the time I returned to the States, I was hired by my university to teach summer Swahili courses.

What made me go from sounding like an infant to being capable of teaching the language? How did the university even know to hire me? It was the maturing process brought about by being immersed in a culture that spoke Swahili. And the university knew to hire me by evaluating my marks of maturity in Swahili.

Being equipped as a disciple of Jesus using a discipleship pathway is very similar to language learning. It requires people to grow from infancy to maturity, becoming proficient in imitating Jesus by being immersed in the way of Jesus. And we as leaders will know if our community and congregation are growing as disciples of Jesus by looking for marks of maturity.

FORMATION FOR MISSION

Discipleship is about formation for mission. The *missio Dei* sends the *imago Dei*; the missional God sends his image-bearers out to renew all things for the sake of the world. Greg McKinzie, a missionary in Arequipa, Peru, writes regarding the *missio Dei*, "Many churches have begun to advocate a vision of 'shalom' or total well-being on a global, societal scale in conjunction with the church's vital participation in God's realization of that reality, which is called the kingdom of God."[1] The theologian Karl Barth notes, "The missionary movement of which we are a part has its source in the triune God himself. . . . We who have been chosen in Christ . . . are by these very facts committed to full participation in his redeeming mission to the world. There is no participation in Christ without participation in his mission to the world."[2] David Bosch adds in *Transforming Mission*, "Mission is a multifaceted ministry, in respect of witness, service, justice, healing, reconciliation, liberation, peace, evangelism, fellowship, church planting, contextualization, and much more. . . . There is church because there is mission."[3] Discipleship is about formation for mission because we are imitating Christ into mission.

The key to discipleship is this: do you imitate Christ in a way that bears kingdom fruit? Are the people you are discipling imitating Christ in a way that bears kingdom fruit?

> I am the vine; you are the branches. If you remain in me and I in you, you
> will bear much fruit; apart from me you can do nothing. (Jn 15:5)

Abiding in Christ, imitating Jesus, and being formed as a disciple are deeply connected to bearing kingdom fruit. Imitating the character of Jesus leads to imitating the praxis of Jesus. Being formed as a disciple of Christ means we follow Christ in his mission for renewal.

Years ago I had gathered a group of twenty-four church leaders in a room to begin a discussion on what discipleship could look like in our church community. The room was full of faithful people who had been "churched" for most of their lives—committed Sunday morning volunteers, small group leaders, deacons, and elders glad to be having fellowship with one another in that living room. We had finished eating together when the dynamics changed with a single question: "Have you ever been discipled?" The chatter stopped and people avoided eye contact.

We waited a long time before one woman had the courage to start. Leslee was a soft-spoken middle school math teacher who shared that she had never been discipled before in her life, so there would be no way for her to disciples others. She didn't know enough, especially about the Bible. She felt insecure and doubtful about her place there in that meeting. She broke down and started to cry. She felt as if she wasn't worthy to be there.

Leslee was not alone in her feelings. No single person in that room could definitively say if they had been discipled. Furthermore, no single person in the room could definitively say if they had discipled anyone else. There was confusion. There was shame. These people needed clarity not only on what being discipled meant but on what discipling others looked like.

Over the following six months, I divided the leaders into two closed groups—meaning we would not add anyone to the group for the duration of this specific discipleship journey—and began to gain clarity with them using a discipleship pathway. As Dan White Jr. says, "Discipleship is becoming proficient in the essentials in order to live into God's in-breaking kingdom."[4] Discipleship is imitating Jesus and, therefore, becoming immersed in the ways of Jesus for the sake of the world. Each closed group of men and women met twice a month to grow and live into the discipleship pathway. While learning and equipping were happening, each man and woman also practiced discipling others using the same discipleship pathway. Where we once had leaders who'd never experienced clear discipleship nor clearly discipled others, we found ourselves with more than a hundred people in a variety of groups discipling and being discipled into the maturity of Christ.

In order to implement a discipleship pathway, we need to have clarity on its purpose. This is crucial.

MATURITY IN CHRIST

Discipleship is about maturity in Christ. The purpose of using a discipleship pathway is to develop mature imitators of Jesus living together in the ways of Jesus for the sake of the world. Maturity can present itself in a variety of ways, but if we were to whittle it down to four essential marks of being transformed by Christ, they would be:

- character
- theology
- wisdom
- missional living

While some may argue, "Why these four?" I offer these four marks of maturity for three reasons. First, each person is impacted by directly imitating Jesus. Therefore they also can be impacted by something else or some other god. Jesus addresses competing loves when he says, "No one can serve two masters. Either you will hate the one and love the other, or you will be devoted to the one and despise the other" (Mt 6:24).

Second, they are distinguishable from "tools" for discipleship but can be developed from tools and practices (such as prayer, evangelism, Scripture reading, etc.). Jesus addresses religiosity and empty practices by highlighting the fruit a person bears in their life:

> He replied [to the Pharisees and teachers of the law], "Isaiah was right when he prophesied about you hypocrites; as it is written:
>
> "'These people honor me with their lips,
>   but their hearts are far from me.
> They worship me in vain;
>   their teachings are merely human rules.' . . .
>
> "Listen to me, everyone, and understand this. Nothing outside a person can defile them by going into them. Rather, it is what comes out of a person that defiles them." (Mk 7:6-7, 14-16)

Third, they cannot be teased apart from one another and stay compartmentalized. In defining the character of love, Jesus binds it to a way of living, saying, "Greater love has no one than this: to lay down one's life for one's friends" (Jn 15:13). The entire Sermon on the Mount emphasizes that upstanding character is not tied just to morality or abstaining from bad behavior; instead, character is bound to actively participating in missional living (Mt 5–7). Wisdom cannot be teased apart from character nor theology from maturing in missional living.

Maturity in character is about the inner person; it's evident in how a person is transformed by the Holy Spirit to be faithful and full of faith, servant-hearted, a lover of God and of others, a peacemaker, full of humility, hospitality, generosity, and joy. They live out the fruit of the Spirit (Gal 5:22-23; Col 3:12) with self-awareness, not out of performance but out of allegiance to Christ.[5] Maturity of character is not the result of inward, private self-help improvement but of the sanctifying, inside-out transformational work of the Holy Spirit, which produces redemptive environments not just for those growing in character but for everyone around them.

Maturity in theology grows out of a continual love of knowing God and being known by God. It's evident in a person "whose delight is in the law of the LORD, and who meditates on his law day and night" (Ps 1:2). Theology is not just about acquiring a wealth of information; it's about knowing God in a way that transforms a person's heart to worship and reorient their life. Maturity in theology is growth in learning about God, but it is also growth in learning to think, love, and do like God and having the "mind of Christ" (1 Cor 2:11-16). Thinking, loving, and acting on behalf of others like God. Thinking about the things that consume God's thoughts. Loving and extending compassion to those God loves and shows compassion to.

Maturity in wisdom is, as Tim Keller says, "competence with regard to the complex realities of life."[6] It shows in the person who develops skills to navigate life well and in the way of Jesus. How do they approach conflict and differences? How do they respond to times of both injustice and providence? How do they balance truth and love, justice and mercy? How do they humbly invite wise counsel and community into their personal and communal decisions? How do they make everyday decisions that demonstrate Jesus' love to the world? Maturity in wisdom shows in how Christ Jesus is becoming wisdom for them (1 Cor 1:26-31).

And finally, maturity in missional living is about a person engaging with the culture around them compelled by the love of Christ (see 2 Cor 5:14-15). It shows in partnering with and being aware of God's work of renewal in the neighborhoods and networks around them. Karl Hartenstein writes, "Mission is not just the conversion of the individual, nor just obedience to the word of the Lord, nor just the obligation to gather the church. It is the taking part in the sending of the Son, the *missio Dei*, with the holistic aim of establishing Christ's rule over all redeemed creation."[7] Missional theologian Lesslie Newbigin adds, "I think that the deepest motive for mission is simply the desire to be with Jesus where he is, on the frontier between the reign of God and the usurped dominion of the devil."[8] Maturity in missional living is evident in how a person understands their partnership in the gospel, both in a personal and gathered rhythm. It shows in how they participate in a community that is being formed for mission together.

Maturity in Christ is the kingdom fruit we're all looking for.

CLEAR ESSENTIALS FOR CLEAR DISCIPLESHIP

Discipleship needs clear essentials. Maturity in character, theology, wisdom, and missional living are clear ways to begin to craft the essentials of a discipleship pathway. What are the essentials required for a disciple and imitator of Jesus to mature into bearing this kind of kingdom fruit? How does a discipleship pathway work?

If you know what maturity, or fruit, looks like, then you need to be clear about what you want people to become immersed in so they can bear that kind of fruit. What are the five to eight essentials you want every person in your church community to grow in so they will actively bear fruit and mature in Christ for the sake of the world? What are the five to eight essentials that will clearly equip your people to be deeply formed in mission together? Clarity in the essentials is key.

Table 3.1. Marks of maturity clarify discipleship essentials

Essential	Tool	Maturity
		Character
		Theology
		Wisdom
		Missional living

A discipleship pathway helps you to have clarity in the essentials so that the tools (methods, programs, equipping, teaching, training models, etc.) for praxis are not just about learning something new but transforming into a new way of living. What are the essentials of discipleship in your church?

We'll dive deeper into concretely developing clear essentials for a discipleship pathway in the next section, but let's first consider the second of Dallas Willard's pivotal questions regarding discipleship: What is our plan for discipleship? And is our plan working?[9]

MIRRORS FOR QUALITY CONTROL

How do we know our plan for discipleship is working? How do we assess the effectiveness of our discipleship pathway? How do we know that the essentials we want to instill in those following Jesus are the "correct" ones?

In our technologically advanced society, we are inundated with non-curated information upon information. We have access to thousands of content sources on "discipleship," and yet most of us and most of those we love and lead fail to live out discipleship—whether being discipled ourselves or discipling others. Even if we compile marks of maturity within our own church communities, how do we know a discipleship pathway will work?

As we journey together in discipleship, we need to be leaders who take on the form of Christ and embark with humility. It takes humility to be able to hold a mirror up to the pathways we construct. We must constantly shape and reshape, sharpen and pivot, depending on where our people are at and what the Holy Spirit is doing in our midst. While the marks of maturity in a discipleship pathway (character, theology, wisdom, and missional living) will not change, other elements—our tools, the order in which we proceed, how we equip disciples together in the essentials—will.

There are three ways to constantly bring a mirror to the discipleship pathway we construct: the fivefold gifts, the three elements of ecclesia, and locally rooted context.

The fivefold gifts. Ephesians 4 displays a clear picture of how maturity in Christ is practically attained:

> So Christ himself gave the apostles, the prophets, the evangelists, the [shepherds] and teachers, to equip his people for works of service, so that the body of Christ may be built up until we all reach unity in the faith and in the knowledge of the Son of God and become mature, attaining to the whole measure of the fullness of Christ. (Eph 4:11-13)

In order to make mature disciples of Jesus, the church is gifted with the fivefold people gifts of apostles, prophets, evangelists, shepherds (pastors), and teachers (APEST). And if maturity is achieved through these gifts, then each of the fivefold perspectives is vital to shaping and equipping disciples through a discipleship pathway.[10] The APEST gifts help equip the whole body of Christ to be a full reflection of Christ. Otherwise, our discipleship will be painfully skewed.

Table 3.2. How the fivefold gifts help the community

Fivefold gift	Focal concern	Telos (destination)
Apostle	Thriving: Living out our calling	Helping the community step out into new territory, living out their "sentness" in their personal spheres of influence by multiplying disciples, ministries, and missional communities
Prophet	Liberating: Pursuing God's shalom	Helping the group pursue God, experience liberation from personal and social sins, and stand with the poor and oppressed in the power of the Spirit
Evangelist	Welcoming: Incarnating the gospel	Helping the community extend the table of fellowship to all, especially those society has marginalized, by being witnesses of his great love
Shepherd	Healing: Seeking wholeness and holiness	Helping people embody reconciliation as well as work through their past hurts and move into a sense of wholeness in the context of community
Teacher	Learning: Inhabiting the Word of God	Helping the community inhabit God's story in such a way that the community teaches one another what it means to live into God's future in an everyday way

When our community first started a discipleship pathway together, we learned about the APEST gifts and split up the room by gift types. Our particular community was mostly divided evenly among evangelists, shepherds, and teachers, with a smattering of prophets and a single apostle. The tensions we were about to encounter were inevitable, and I knew our discipleship pathway had to include a way for all five APEST gifts to be understood and utilized in order for maturity to happen.

We were busily preparing for our first ever community dinner, called Open Spaces, which was open to anyone, especially our non-Jesus-following guests. We would soon be in a room with potluck dishes covering the table, busy engaging with our families, friends, coworkers, and neighbors, sharing a meal and sharing our stories together. But more importantly, we needed to be prepared to understand and utilize the APEST gifts to grow in our maturity as disciples. Through a simple exercise, each fivefold representative was able to articulate how they might feel during the community dinner and how they could uniquely connect to Jesus to help them mature as a committed disciple.

Table 3.3. Fivefold feelings and commitments

Fivefold gift	I may feel . .	I commit to . . .
Apostle	Antsy. It will feel like no movement or multiplication of people is happening, and that feels slow and frustrating for me.	Being patient. I will connect with Jesus knowing that his kingdom is on the move and that it often starts small and slow before growing exponentially.
Prophet	Grumpy. It will feel like we aren't doing anything meaningful to address social injustice issues.	Being gentle. I will connect with Jesus knowing that his kingdom is always issuing righteousness through his people who are experiencing community life together.
Evangelist	Anxious. Open Spaces dinner may not be full of new people and outsiders.	Loving my shepherd-gifted brothers and sisters and being mindful of how they'll be thinking and feeling as our community starts off. I'll learn to focus on the needs of those on the inside versus those on the outside for now.
Shepherd	Threatened. Open Spaces dinner may be too full of new people and outsiders, and not everyone will get a chance to feel connected for the long haul.	Thinking of the short game. I'll love, guard, and guide the people who are present here now just for this evening. The next dinner will be a reset.
Teacher	Like we're doing things incorrectly. It may feel like we're not purposefully connecting people to God's truth and the Bible.	Living out how Jesus connected people to himself as the incarnate Word by connecting them to God's Word through my regular conversations at Open Spaces, instead of thinking it needs to happen on a larger platform up front.

Imagine a discipleship pathway that only values learning and the teacher gift; it will be skewed to telling your community that only those who know the Bible well are active followers of Jesus. If a discipleship pathway only highlights the evangelist's heart of hospitality and welcome, the community will quickly learn to have only shallow relationships in order to never threaten welcome. If the shepherd's focal concern for healing trumps the discipleship pathway, the community will get smaller as depth of relationship among a small group of people always feels more valuable than growth. If the pathway skews toward the prophet, the community will only value mission in terms of social justice instead of including welcome and a sense of belonging. And if the apostle's telos is seen as most important, the community will participate in a hundred different things without establishing a culture of faithfulness and welcome.

The world needs a community full of disciples who mature in learning, reconciliation, incarnation, liberation, and kingdom partnership. Our discipleship pathways should reflect what each fivefold gift brings to the table to reflect the fullness of Christ.

Does your discipleship pathway reflect the telos or destination of each fivefold gift? How does your discipleship pathway mature disciples into concerns of:

- learning to inhabit the Word of God?
- reconciliation to the wholeness and holiness of community?
- incarnational hospitality?
- liberation toward God's shalom?
- living into the sentness of the kingdom of God?

Who might you need to invite into the process of developing a discipleship pathway in order to better reflect all fivefold gifts?

Three elements of ecclesia. When we think of the rules and rhythms of the church, what do we picture? If we were to shave down the practices of a group of disciples, we can simplify it to three elements of the church:

- communion—a deep personal connection with God
- community—a deep communal connection with others
- co-mission—a deep work of renewal for the culture (neighborhoods and networks) around us

As Woodward and White note, "This is the essence of the church: a people who find their identity in the arms of God (communion), rallied around tables welcoming each other (community) and sent out into the world with serving hands (co-mission)."[11] The practices and rhythm of a discipleship pathway orient around communion, community and co-mission. A discipleship pathway centers around our identities becoming reoriented toward who God is and what he does for the sake of the world around us.

In our community, we incorporate these three elements of the church in terms of formation, community, and renewal. We think about these elements in light of Deb Hirsch's insightful questions regarding community life:[12]

- Who am I? (identity, formation, communion)
- Where am I going? (purpose, renewal, co-mission)
- Who am I going with? (community)

Our discipleship pathway and its rule and rhythm help us engage in the deep work of our personal connection with God, our communal connection with others (including both Jesus-followers and non-Jesus-followers), and our active participation in the work of renewal for the culture around us.

Melissa, who is now one of our missional community leaders, engaged in our discipleship pathway by maturing in communion, community, and co-mission. She practiced communion by immersing herself in a dedicated weekly time to connect with God through experiencing nature and his creation. Without fail, hiking in the Koʻolau mountains or swimming at Kailua beach instantly brought her to tears and helped her pray to God, who had before often felt distant. She practiced community by sticking with her fellow disciples and participating in providing a weekly community dinner for our guests, which often helped her see a better reflection of Jesus' friendship. And she practiced co-mission by growing a heart for the houseless community in her own neighborhood, starting a missional community center around including those in need as a vital and dignified part of their neighborhood. Discipleship includes connection with God, commitment to others, and mission for renewal.

- How does your discipleship pathway include communion, community, and co-mission?
- How does your discipleship pathway allow disciples to practice both a personal rhythm and a gathered rhythm?
- What evidence of maturity are you looking for that tells you disciples are growing in communion (identity, formation), community (gathered rhythm), and co-mission (purpose, renewal)?

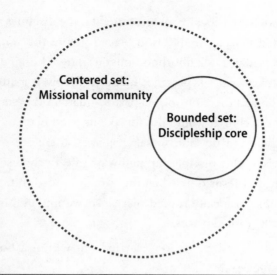

Figure 3.1. Locally rooted context requires a bounded set within the centered set

Locally rooted context. Discipleship cannot happen without a community of disciples invested in a real-life local context. If a discipleship pathway is all about maturing disciples into the likeness of Jesus, then formation does not occur without mission. All the equipping and formational work of a discipleship pathway is carried out most effectively through a bounded set within a centered set—in other words, a discipleship core (a closed group of disciples living out a discipleship pathway together) within a missional community (an open community where all are invited to participate in a sense of belonging and of purpose right in their own local neighborhood or network).

A discipleship pathway works best for a bounded set/closed group of disciples who are committed to Jesus and to one another. And it's pivotal that these disciples live into mission in their local context and for the sake of their local context.

This third mirror for quality control—which helps us answer the question, "Is our plan for discipleship working?"—is probably the reflector we should visit over and over again. If the church is not locally rooted, then the work of local renewal will never really happen. At best it will be event-based, episodic, and unsustainable. A discipleship pathway cannot have a locally rooted context if the disciples aren't set in a locally rooted place. The question placed before the church should always be, "Would our neighborhood miss us if our church didn't exist?"

Wherever Jesus went, his presence mattered deeply. It mattered to that local place if he was there or not. As pastor Jonathan Brooks states, "My prayer is that the church would not forsake its local place. . . . We know clearly that there are no God-forsaken places; there are only church-forsaken places."[13] Our discipleship pathways effectively disciple people into the likeness of Jesus only when they are grounded in the truth that Jesus met people in locally rooted places, so we imitate him by being present in locally rooted places.

- Is your discipleship pathway carried out within a bounded set/ discipleship core?
- Is that core tethered to a centered set/missional community?
- How does your discipleship pathway bring about a sense of belonging for the centered set/missional community?
- How does it bring about a sense of purpose for the centered set/ missional community?

A discipleship pathway develops essentials of maturity for disciples in character, theology, wisdom, and missional living. But a disciple must mature through the way of Jesus; that is, discipleship reflects the fullness of Christ through the fivefold gifts of apostles, prophets, evangelist, shepherds, and teachers within the elements of ecclesia, communion, community, and co-mission, lived out practically with a discipleship core (a bounded set) tethered to a missional community (a centered set).

Within the first six months of starting a discipleship pathway together, Leslee, our timid middle school math teacher, started to find her own story within God's story. She not only grew a sense of confidence but began sharing the gospel with her family and friends. She shared with her mother; she shared with her teenage son; she shared with her closest friends since high school. She even shared with a friend who had recently been diagnosed with stage four cancer and began to have regular, intimate faith conversations with her.

Leslee didn't stop there. As she continued to mature in the likeness of Christ, she started a Christian student group at school after a recent mandate had banned outside parachurch organizations from meeting on campus. Leslee intentionally imitated Jesus, and he invited her to partner in his redeeming work for her friendships, family, neighborhood, and workplace.

Leslee followed Jesus.

PART 2

DEVELOPING A DISCIPLESHIP PATHWAY

*One who is "in Christ" acts in ways that
demonstrate that transformed identity.*

HALEY GORANSON JACOB

4

FROM PAST RECIPES
TO LOCAL CUISINE

*For whatever reason, God now reveals himself in the world
not through a pillar of smoke and fire, not even through
the physical body of his Son in Galilee, but through
the mongrel collection that comprises my local church
and every other such gathering in God's name.*

PHILIP YANCEY

*We no longer believe just because of what you said;
now we have heard for ourselves, and we know that
this man really is the Savior of the world.*

JOHN 4:42

YOU KNOW YOU'RE GETTING a proper Philly cheesesteak by how it's presented to you. If it has neatly sliced bright-green lettuce strips gingerly placed around the golden-brown meat topped by gourmet Gruyère inside a freshly baked sprouted-seed-bespeckled homemade roll, it's not a Philly cheesesteak. If the server haphazardly launches a plate at you bearing an Amoroso's white bread hoagie roll, chopped-up steak mixed with fried white onions, and yellow American cheese slices, and after just a moment the red-checkered paper tablecloth is immediately stained with grease— yeah, that's a Philly cheesesteak.

I was born in Seoul, South Korea, immigrated to and was raised in West Philadelphia, and migrated in the last decade to Honolulu, Hawaii. So my sense of local cuisine has changed, but I know a Philly cheesesteak when I see one. I ordered a Philly cheesesteak once in Hawaii—big mistake. Too much teriyaki. I had a Philly cheesesteak in a fancy burger joint once—too much fancy seasoning. In my desperation for a taste of home, I even ordered a Philly cheesesteak in Paris. Too French. The only way to satisfy my Philly appetite for a Philly cheesesteak is to stay local and order local.

My older brother owned a small corner grocery store in North Philadelphia, and in my mind, Pat's or Gino's had nothing on him. He was slopping and chopping steak, fake cheese slices, and anemic diced onions twelve hours straight on that massive stove and was a local cheesesteak hero. All the neighbors came for "John's steak." Nearby business owners and corner store workers stopped by on their lunch breaks for John's steak. In lieu of donuts, the local Philly cops stopped by on their routine patrol for John's steak. My parents would stop by weekly to drop off my brother's mail and in return got a bag full of his steaks—wrapped, of course, in butcher paper, the grease already leaking through.

Local cuisine is just that—it's food that's made locally. It incorporates local flavors and houses local memories. It invites local gatherings and local conversations. Local cuisine celebrates a rootedness in local culture, and when out of place or improperly imitated, it's not familiar. When you have a Philly cheesesteak in the city of brotherly love, you're enjoying the best local culture provides.

It's no different when developing a discipleship pathway. A locally curated and lovingly belabored discipleship pathway that comes out of a locally rooted church and community does so for the development of local disciples in a way a cookie cutter model of discipleship cannot accomplish. We'll explore common cookie cutter models of discipleship, what local cuisine can look like, and end with examples of local fare.

PAST RECIPES

Discipleship is immersed within a community where praxis happens in the context of local neighborhood or network renewal. If we continue our cuisine analogy, developing a discipleship pathway for our uniquely local churches and communities does not mean we take a past recipe and copy it. Local cuisine can borrow and learn from past recipes, but developing local cuisine means we intentionally incorporate local flavor and curate local intelligence. Localized discipleship involves a locally rooted group of disciples for the sake of a locally rooted place.

My husband, Steve, is in no sense what you would confidently call a chef. It was in our first year of marriage that he first peeled both an orange (yes!) and a hard-boiled egg (again, yes!). In our twenty years of marriage his cuisine work started off with learning to use simple kitchen utensils and develop simple skills, and it plateaued for a while at meticulously following recipes. His process was as such: Print out recipe—check. Read step one—check. Do step one—check. Read step two—check. And so on and so forth. And, yes, he literally took a pen and checked off each step as he carefully navigated through the list of steps.

With his earlier meals our family would eat three hours later than usual not because difficult French cuisine had been laid before us but because every step of a basic recipe felt meticulous and detailed for my husband to master. But more recently, because of a rhythm of weekly dinner making, a commitment to mastering a short list of recipes (his go-to is Indian), and having a well-stocked spice pantry, Steve has started not only to cook without a printed recipe but to taste the food for a seasoning of his liking, experiment with different Indian spices, and ring the dinner bell just thirty minutes after start time. Steve learned the art of starting off with a past recipe but now enjoys the creativity of making it his own.

In my coaching and consulting work with various leaders and pastors, most pastors are drawn to a copycat approach and following recipes precisely, much like how Steve started out. The mistake isn't in trying out past recipes; the mistake lies in not making it our own local cuisine with local flavors for local people.

In our day and age of sharp denominational disputes among the Christian diaspora (along with emerging postmillennial thought, disagreements on power dynamics in church leadership, past and current leadership scandals, and the church's engagement or lack thereof in politics),[1] we are also coming to a head as a culture in confronting the pervasiveness of White evangelicalism and its overreaching extensions (along with the debris it has left behind in its equally overreaching wake). Developing local discipleship is not a creative exercise of contemporary Christian leadership—it is a necessary response to how Christendom has taken shape within culture.

While White evangelicalism is not the same thing as white supremacy, it would be a crying shame not to admit to some underlying ties. As Tim Keller says in his critical book *Center Church*, "If we are not deliberately thinking about our culture, we will simply be conformed to it without ever knowing it is happening."[2] And as Isabel Wilkerson expertly writes in her seminal book *Caste*, "Caste [or our current social hierarchical ladder] is insidious and therefore powerful because it is not hatred, it is not necessarily personal. It is the worn grooves of comforting routines and unthinking expectations, patterns of a social order that have been in place for so long that it looks like the natural order of things."[3]

The sad but exposed truth about the church today is that we have been conformed to and comfortable with the present-day and historical enmeshment of colonialism and Christendom. Even as we approach the beautiful work of developing a discipleship pathway in our local and current contexts, wise leaders acknowledge and grow in humble awareness that we are also doing the messy work of deconstructing and decolonizing discipleship.

LOCAL CUISINE

Because I am Korean American (100 percent purebred with milky Korean skin and jet-black hair), my skin turns quintessentially golden-brown in Hawaii's sun. Because my husband is German American (100 percent purebred with pale white skin and jet-red hair), his skin turns undeniably angry red in Hawaii's sun. Thankfully, our *hapa* (meaning "half-half" or "mixed" in Hawaiian) children pulled toward golden-brown and away from angry red. Because of my golden-brown skin, all the locals think I'm local and I happened to marry *haole* (meaning "outsider"), but as soon as I open my Philly mouth, everyone looks past the tanness of my skin and labels me *haole*. Ironically, when Steve opens his mouth and begins to draw a comfortable crowd of local folks around him, people start to look past the paleness of his skin and give him an inside pass.

The difference in what comes out of our mouths makes all the difference in who gets instantly accepted and who doesn't, and I had a steeper learning curve than Steve. He naturally knew the art of *wala'au* (meaning "talking story"), having grown up in rural Pennsylvania in a farming community. Country folk speak country folk, and apparently, you'll pick up the cultural language quicker if your sense of place shares a similar root. People like to slow down here and take time to catch up and hear about each other's goings on, even if it happens to start with the weather or surf report. My husband genuinely has the knack for this, while I, on the other hand, do not. My talking story ability was poor a decade ago, and it's only improved a smidge since then, because growing up on the East Coast means I talk fast, I walk fast, and I just everything fast. I had to learn the language of slowing down in order for my voice to be heard. I don't necessarily change what I want to say, but I change the way I say it.

In order for us as leaders to develop effective discipleship pathways unique to our local cultural contexts, we need to be able to balance two points that seem to be in contention with each other: common universal discipleship essentials and unique local expressions of discipleship. What we're saying and how we say it are important. We want to equip our people to mature more into the beautiful likeness of Christ, and how we go about equipping them in a unique local context matters. We cannot focus just on common universal discipleship essentials, and we also cannot focus just on unique local expressions of discipleship.

THE PROBLEM WITH UNIVERSAL DISCIPLESHIP MODELS

The problem with focusing only on common universal discipleship models is that, just like past recipes, they're meant to be improved on. We use these models as a launching point and helpful framework, not as inflexible dogma or doctrine. We learn from and practice our own discipleship through them, especially if discipleship is new to us. The best universal models are the ones that help leaders connect and piece together unique aspects of their own communities and cultures. The best models also help keep the holistic nature of discipleship in mind.

At the same time, the best models have a flexibility and openness that allow them to be tested in unique local spaces, with an understanding that no discipleship tool is one-size-fits-all. A worthwhile model moves away from becoming formulaic or programmatic, and its feasibility is not based on a higher level of expertise or skillset. The best universal discipleship models help launch holistic discipleship pathways for local communities, allow and even expect the local community to improve and deeply shape them, and are easily scalable and reproducible in a variety of settings. Most importantly, the best universal discipleship models are not antiquated forms of colonial practices where one culture displaces another in the name of Jesus.

Table 4.1. Limitations with universal discipleship models

Universal discipleship models too often:
Let themselves go untested in the local space
Incorporate antiquated practices from colonialism
Take a one-size-fits-all approach
Become programmatic and wrongly metric-based
Build leadership credibility based on the expertise of the designer

Upon perusing Western Christian publishers (e.g., InterVarsity Press, Zondervan, and Eerdmans) and searching sites such as Amazon, Google, and Bing using "bestsellers in Christian discipleship" and similar phrases, I made four key observations about the resources available to church leaders and everyday Christians alike who are looking for a practical discipleship pathway model:

1. Most resources on the topic of discipleship are based on a self-improvement/self-help model (often addressed separately to male, female, or youth) or on counseling methods focusing on character and morality.

2. Most resources look to build up a biblical background or historical knowledge in discussing discipleship but lack practical next steps for

people to actively participate in real-time discipleship today (which often results in discipleship being about how much information someone knows or reserving discipleship for those with a strong theological background).

3. Most resources look at different aspects of discipleship, such as learning the biblical story, cultivating an evangelistic or apologetic lifestyle, or addressing issues of sanctification, but they rarely connect the dots to see discipleship as the main way to mature fully in the image of Jesus (through concrete marks of a mature missional disciple).

4. Most resources (apart from those in gender-specific self-improvement genres) are written by male Caucasian paid church leaders. There is a large void of discipleship materials presented from a female, BIPOC, covocational, or church practitioner point of view.

While the above observations on discipleship resources aren't bad per se, the problem is that universal discipleship models are gravely skewed and limited.

THE PROBLEM WITH LOCAL EXPRESSIONS OF DISCIPLESHIP MODELS

On the other hand, the problem with focusing only on unique local expressions of discipleship is that without a common framework to launch from, these unique expressions aren't as holistic and sustainable as we would hope them to be. They're also often tied and limited to the gift sets of the originating leader or based on a cultural or relational longevity that's hard to catch up to. While universal common models may be too formulaic, uniquely local expressions may be too organic. The more formulaic a model, the less realistic and relatable it is; the more organic a model, the less reproducible and sustainable it is. Unique local expressions of discipleship that are not integrated with a common discipleship framework also are often more influenced by the local culture than they influence the local culture; most of the time they will choose to appease rather than offend.

Table 4.2. Limitations with local expressions of discipleship

Unique local expressions of discipleship too often:
Miss a holistic frame
Are more influenced by the local culture than influencing the local culture
Actively react to colonialism
Are not sustainable since resources aren't collected and measured
Build credibility based on the social influence of the practitioner

How do we hold both of these values not only in tension but in collaboration? This is where a discipleship pathway is immensely important. As we take a deeper dive in the next two chapters on building a foundation for a discipleship pathway, we'll keep in mind how to keep both a universal common discipleship framework and a uniquely local expression of discipleship in balance.

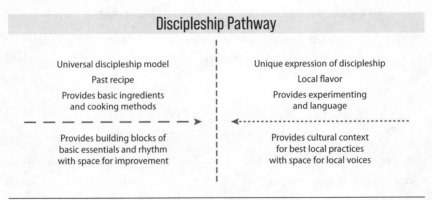

Figure 4.1. Using both universal models and local expressions of discipleship.

Just as every recipe, however uniquely local it is, has basic culinary essentials (either ingredients or cooking method), every discipleship pathway in its uniquely local expressions also has basic discipleship essentials. The building blocks we'll look at to scaffold our unique discipleship pathway involve both the journey and the essentials of discipleship. The journey (as we'll see in chapter six) includes ways to make our discipleship pathway, however locally contextualized, meaningful, formational, communal, renewal, and rhythmic. Essentials (as we'll pursue in chapter five) involve clear marks of maturity, the core competencies that will move our people toward maturity, and the tools that help connect the two.

CULTURAL CONTEXT MATTERS

Remember the Hawaiian concept of *wala'au* (talking story) and how it helped my husband connect more easily to our local context here? Well, it isn't just a way to shoot the breeze with people; it actually is a meaningful way of forming deep relational trust. A friend of mine who works for the Centers for Disease Control and Prevention (CDC) happens to be a Caucasian woman who was born and raised in Hawaii but looks like an outsider. Before moving back home to Oahu, Krista had been stationed at the main campus in Atlanta. She ended up getting assigned to a small CDC team that went to Hawaii to investigate a potentially new disease (no, it wasn't Covid). The assignment entailed inspections and groundwork at the local airport, which was under the jurisdiction of the local CDC manager, who happened to be a local Polynesian man. The Atlanta-based investigators were excited to be in Hawaii and eager to start the research. They expected a concise welcome and briefing from the local manager before they launched into their on-site work.

The first day went by and the manager did not give an assignment to any one of the Atlanta investigators. They sat in his office, and he was cordial and friendly, talking story like the best local Hawaiian culture could offer, but the one thing that did not happen was site placement. Another day went by and then another. Most of the out-of-state workers were frustrated, rolling their eyes, trying to figure out how to be productive and complete the assignment without being assigned a placement. But Krista, who looked like all the other White agents, came in every day to the manager's office, sat by him, and talked story with him. She was born and raised in Hawaii; she too knew how to *wala'au*.

Sure enough, after three days of hearing local stories, the team received a placement. But instead of assigning the entire Atlanta team for the site investigation, the CDC manager sent only one person: Krista, who had spent time building a foundation of trust with her local manager.

If we as leaders are going to develop a discipleship pathway that is locally rooted, then cultural context matters. Knowing how relational trust is established in a community helps us know how to equip our people for mature ways of relating to one another and being family within that local place. Knowing how local people learn helps us know what kinds of tools will equip them in ways that apply to their real lives. Knowing how people engage with their neighborhoods and communities, what rhythms of the city people follow, and what community events are meaningful to people helps us know where the best spaces are for incarnational discipleship.

The best way of infusing local flavors is to use local ingredients. The best way to develop a discipleship pathway that is culturally contextual is to use local "ingredients" of the community: knowing the local culture and knowing the locals. Developing a discipleship pathway that is locally rooted cannot omit an exegesis of the neighborhood (or network), listening to local and native voices, or a deference to local leadership.

STORIES OF LOCAL CUISINE

I sat around a fire pit in a predominantly White neighborhood in Portland, Oregon, encircled by a welcoming and generous group of local disciples, each wrestling individually with their own faith assumptions and connections to Jesus but each equally emboldened and challenged by current issues of social inequity and lack of inclusiveness. While sitting in a White majority crowd and being the only minority in the proverbial room, I had never felt so supported as a female leader. The Holy Spirit was doing a deeply local work in this burgeoning progressive group of women and men as they contended with gender inequality. Their localized discipleship pathway included confronting power dynamics as they learned what it meant to be a follower of Jesus.

In another gathering, I sat with a young Black bivocational pastor who had grown up and lived and loved in Camden, New Jersey, and had been faithfully ministering to his long-standing congregation and neighborhood for years. In their localized discipleship pathway everyone sat in a circle, young and old, and while there was a bit of equipping and teaching involved, the leader knew that the deepest sense of communion happened in the first hour of setting up metal folding chairs in the community hall, with every person sharing their story about work, family, a walk to the grocery store, school—whatever the story was, it was about something connected to the neighborhood they all lived and loved in. Their discipleship held a space for local stories.

I have also sat in a virtual room with a group of local disciples, who all happen to be White, rooted in Big Lake, Minnesota, who have grown together in their journey of intentionally being neighbors to the people living immediately next door to them. Their discipleship pathway highlighted interdependence within a community, and the biggest thing they were trying to resist was the culture of individualism and consumerism. The Holy Spirit was doing a deep local work of transforming these individual followers of Jesus from privatized Christians into a community of Jesus-followers. They actively displayed to the neighborhood around them who Jesus is by their intentional and interdependent love for one another.

On another occasion I sat with an older Black leader who's like the mayor of his pocket neighborhood in Brooklyn, where arts meet project homes meet health initiatives. He leads and loves a group of disciples who come from dramatically different backgrounds given the nature of New York City, but each person is committed to the ways Jesus deals with holistic health, attentiveness to the city, creative arts, and justice around diversity and equity. Their discipleship pathway matures this core group of people to think about these topics of passion through the lens of the gospel—what does holistic health mean to God and what does it look like for us in our city? What do creative arts mean to God and what do they look like for us in our city? What does justice around diversity and equity mean to God and what do they look like for us in our city? Their discipleship pathway deals straight-on with the works of justice they encounter daily in Brooklyn.

Each of these local cuisines all developed from the same recipe. Each localized discipleship pathway came from the same work entered into by each leader. And each leader knew how to infuse local flavors into their discipleship pathway because they did the tilling work of exegeting their local place and including local voices.

5

ESSENTIAL INGREDIENTS FOR ANY PATHWAY

*The intention of Jesus was not to leave behind
a disembodied teaching. It was that through his
total consecration to the Father in his passion,
there should be created a community which
would continue that which he came from the
Father to be and to do—namely to embody and
to announce the presence of the reign of God.*

LESSLIE NEWBIGIN

*Therefore, if anyone is in Christ, the new creation
has come: The old has gone, the new is here!*

2 CORINTHIANS 5:17

I USED TO THINK MISSION MEANT sharing the Roman Road to Salvation to a stranger in a foreign land. I had gone on "mission trips," rehearsed my speech, and, on my return flight, resumed my normal life of keeping to myself and my comforts. Missional living and making disciples happened in only foreign countries where missionaries were sent; it didn't happen at home.

Everything changed when I started discipling others.

When I started discipling people, I saw not just their lives change, but their families, friend groups, work places, and neighborhoods start to change. When I started sitting down with people and equipping them in the way of Jesus, the love of Christ started to compel them to go out into their own spheres of influence in their personal lives and bring about the presence of the kingdom of God. When people were discipled, they were sent into mission right where they were.

The Father sends the Son, and together, they send the Spirit for the renewal of all things through the embodiment and announcement of the beauty, power, and transformed life in the kingdom of God. The *missio Dei* sends the *imago Dei* within community. Discipleship is about being a *sent people*. And disciples are sent, in imitating Jesus, to go and make more imitators of Jesus.

Discipleship that seeks to make mature imitators of Jesus (in character, theology, wisdom, and missional living) invites them into a journey where formation for mission happens. In fact, where formation *and* mission happen. A discipleship pathway helps clarify for our community what essentials we will focus on in the life of our church in order to become more like Jesus for the sake of the neighborhood our local community exists within. A simple way of constructing a discipleship pathway in your own church or community is to have a beginning, a middle, and an end.

BEGIN WITH THE END IN MIND

Before we disciple people into the essentials, we must first look for what the Holy Spirit is forming and transforming in their lives. As leaders, we need to know for ourselves what maturity in Christ looks like. Then we look for those marks of maturity that clearly tell us people are becoming disciples and imitators of Jesus. We look for how their character, theology, wisdom, and missional living are becoming more and more conformed to the image of the Son (Rom 8:29).

Table 5.1. Discipleship pathway framework

Beginning	Middle	End
Essentials	*Tools*	*Maturity*
What are the essentials of discipleship in your church?	How are people being equipped in these essentials?	What specific markers are you looking for that tell you people are being equipped in these essentials?
1.	1.	1.
2.	2.	2.
3.	3.	3.
4.	4.	4.
5.	5.	5.

- What specific markers are you are looking for that tell you people are being equipped into the likeness of Christ?
- What stories do you imagine people sharing with one another as they are discipled into maturity?
- What marks of character, theology, wisdom, and missional living do you expect to see in people?
- What marks of maturity do you already see in your church today?
- Who are the people in your community who are already displaying marks of maturity?
- How do you know they are mature?

Once we have clarity on what a mature disciple looks like, then we consider the unique essentials of our church community. The end shapes our essentials. A clear picture of maturity helps us know why we choose our essentials. The essentials in our churches and communities help shape and move people toward the maturity of Christ. We need to be crystal clear about how exactly we are equipping people in order for them to imitate Jesus. Otherwise, there will be a lot of well-intentioned admirers of Jesus instead of intentional imitators of Jesus.[1]

- What are the essentials of discipleship in your church?
- How do those essentials lead to mature disciples of Jesus, in character, theology, wisdom, and missional living?

- What do these essentials say about the vision and values of your church?
- How do these essentials connect people to God, to one another, and to mission?
- How are these essentials already at work in your church?

MANY TOOLS IN THE TOOLBOX

Once we know the essentials of a discipleship pathway and are on the lookout for specific marks of maturity, then we are free to explore and experiment with a variety of tools that can help us equip disciples. Essentials guide us on what to focus on, and marks of maturity let us know if our focus is adrift. The beauty of tools is that their variety allows them to fit all different kinds of people.

For instance, one of the essentials in my church is to have a "heart for the one." A mark of maturity for this essential is that disciples begin to share stories about how they had a conversation with non-Christians about Jesus. When we look at tools, each person in my church uses something a little different. For instance, one person makes it a habit to call her non-Christian friends once a week, every week, to check in on them in the hopes that her consistent presence over the phone will produce conversations about Jesus and new life only found in him. Another person prays every day for a particular coworker and makes it a habit to take a break from work to engage in some meaningful conversation with him. Every day. We use simple tools to identify people who don't know Jesus yet and create intentional rhythms of prayer and presence to share and model the goodness of Jesus. In fact, several people have come to know and love Jesus because of these practices in these disciples' lives.

- How are people in your church being equipped in the essentials?
- What are three tools for each essential that can help people both learn and live into the essentials in their regular rhythms? Write these down.
- How do these tools lead to marks of maturity?
- How have you considered different types of tools for discipling different types of people?
- Are the tools replicable for any disciple to disciple others?

STORY BY EXAMPLE

Because story is one of the best ways to inspire and spark creativity, I'll pause here to describe why and how I landed on the five essentials in our discipleship pathway. I cannot stress enough, though, that this is our unique local cuisine based on our unique locally rooted context, and our discipleship pathway is both a cultural and sustainable artifact for our locally rooted church. For each of the five essentials, I'll share a tool we use to connect the essential to a mark of maturity as we're on the lookout for kingdom fruit with hopeful expectation. And last, keeping leadership in mind, I'll show how each of the five essentials in our discipleship pathway is simple enough that every disciple can understand and internalize it for themselves. The simplicity allows for the discipleship pathway to be replicable. Again, discipleship is meant to be a routine part of our new way of living because of Christ, within a sent community of people on mission together.

Table 5.2. Example of a discipleship pathway: Honolulu, Hawaii

Essential	Tool	Mark of maturity
Full gospel: I know God's story and how my own story fits in	The four acts of God's story	• They can tell us the full gospel in their own words. • By understanding God's story, they ask to understand their own story by being baptized.
True humanity: I know who I am because I am personally connected to Jesus	Low planks	• They start to tell us stories about how God has been speaking to them. • They begin to not recognize themselves, saying things like, "Before I used to _____, but now I find myself _____."
Thick community: I belong to God's unified, growing, and diverse family	Thin versus thick	• They start to talk about people who aren't their blood family like they are their own family. • They tell stories about how they are able to work well with and enjoy others who are different from them. • They tell us stories about how others have helped them and how they have helped others.
Heart for the one: I share with others God's heart of self-giving love	Five alive	• They tell us about people they are personally praying for and reaching out to. • They tell stories about how they're helping others in their immediate contexts to flourish.
Kingdom partnership: I actively participate in the life-giving reign of God	Spaces, places, people	• They can tell us why God has put them where they are in the world and the ways in which he is using them. • They recognize that it is about first seeking God's kingdom before they build their own.

In thinking through the common marks of maturity we desire to see in people who are following Jesus, I started considering the core elements that help bear that kingdom fruit in people. What do people need to know and also practice in order for Christlike character to well up in them? What are the key things people need to be equipped in for Christlike theology to transform and renew our minds? What theme helps us live intentionally and seek after God's wisdom for navigating life? What drives people to be compelled to live missional lives themselves?

As you can see from that list of questions, our community started off with a lot of prayer and a realization that discipleship is, in fact, the work of the Holy Spirit. It's the work of the Holy Spirit that our inner being becomes transformed into the likeness of Christ, where we become people who bear love, joy, peace, patience, kindness, goodness, faithfulness, gentleness, and self-control (Gal 5:22-23) for the sake of those around us. It's the work of the Holy Spirit that renews our minds and allows us to have the mind of Christ himself (1 Cor 2:16). It's the work of the Holy Spirit that Christ himself has become our very wisdom (1 Cor 1:30). And it's the work of the Holy Spirit that sends us out together in community on mission together (Acts 1:8). Discipleship is the work of God and we are invited to participate in this good work.

I arrived on the five essentials of our discipleship pathway through trial and error. There's probably been five different iterations of it over the course of five years, but we only learned what worked, what resonated within our local context, and what began to bear fruit as we just tried and tried. The key elements never changed, but we made adjustments as we discovered what needed to be simplified, what needed clarity, what needed more depth, and what needed to be discarded or added. We utilized the mirrors of quality control (the fivefold gifts, three elements of ecclesia, and locally rooted presence—see chapter three) to work out essentials that addressed everyone as disciples and not just a few. We kept the end in mind while maintaining a close eye on how replicable our discipleship pathway would be.

The tools we use for each discipleship pathway essential have a few common elements:

- Connect us to Scripture
- Connect us to imitation of Jesus

- Connect us to engage in both community and mission
- Connect us to praxis

Our five discipleship pathway essentials are the Full Gospel, True Humanity, Thick Community, Heart for the One, and Kingdom Partnership.

FULL GOSPEL

We always begin with the Full Gospel, because understanding and anchoring our own stories around God's story is pivotal in our current storytelling world. Look around and you'll find story everywhere. And the best stories aren't the ones that download information to you or make you an expert on a given topic—they're the stories that resonate deeply with something in your own spirit or experience. A story about World War II can be shared via a historical textbook, or it can be shared through a story about two brothers experiencing a loss that makes you think about your own connection to family and reflect on your own personal loss.

Story is also important in how it crafts and depicts what's of value to a given culture. Go to any town or city and look at the story it's telling. Go to any friend gathering or family affair and hear the narrative of what's valuable in these relationships. Listen to what's popular on Spotify or YouTube or the latest podcast and you'll hear that culture's account of love and success. Story is how advertising works. It's what grounds the best businesses. Story captures readers and moviegoers. Story is what moves the multibillion-dollar music industry and all entertainment industries. Story is important in culture, and the narrative in our postmodern culture shows our values, loves, and successes. In a discipleship pathway, we want to equip every disciple in our community with God's story and extend his invitation for everyone's story to join his story in a personal and communal way.

One of the tools we use to connect the full gospel essential ("I know God's story and how my own story fits in") to the mark of maturity ("They can tell the full gospel in their own words") is something we call "the four acts of God's story."

We needed a tool that helped our disciples move from a truncated half-gospel to a robust full gospel that addressed two pivotal questions everyone asks: Who am I? And what am I supposed to do? These are the deep questions of identity and purpose. The "four acts of God's story" tool moved them from a narrative that said, "I am a sinner and I'm waiting to go to heaven" to "I am God's image-bearer to be and do good, and I'm partnered with God in the good work of restoring goodness in the world." The four acts tool moves disciples through the complete themes of the gospel:

- Act one: creation. God is good (Ps 119:68; Ps 136:1), God created everything good (Gen 1:1-25), God created you and me good (Gen 1:26-27), and God created you and me to do good (Gen 1:28-31).

- Act two: rebellion. The liar (Satan) thinks God is not good (Is 14:12-15); the liar lies to you and me and says God is not good (Gen 3:1-5); we believe the lie that God is not good (sin) (Gen 3:6-13); believing the lie brings the kingdom of darkness into the world (the effects of sin) (Gen 3:14-24); and believing the lie separates you and me—from God, from each other, and from creation (Rom 3:23).

- Act three: redemption (restoration through sacrifice). Jesus is God (Heb 1:2-3; Jn 1:1-5), Jesus enters the world as a human (incarnation) (Jn 1:14; Lk 2:1-20), Jesus brings the kingdom of God to the world (Mk 1:14-15; Mk 4:30-32), Jesus breaks the lie and separation (crucifixion) (Jn 3:16; Mk 15:33-39; Rom 5:8), and Jesus defeats the power of sin and death (resurrection) (Mk 16:1-7; Rom 6:23).

- Act four: reclaiming (creation reinstated). Remember, God created you and me to do good (Eph 2:10), Jesus tells his friends to partner with him in the kingdom of God (and undo the works of darkness) (1 Jn 3:8), Jesus tells his friends to help break the lie about God (and make disciples) (Mt 28:19-20), the Holy Spirit lives inside you and me to be good and do good (Jn 14:15-17; Acts 2:1-4; Gal 5:22-23), so how are you partnering with Jesus today (Mt 16:24-25; Jn 10:10)?

The tool provides ample space for disciples to articulate the gospel in their own words; in fact, every person who has gone through a discipleship pathway in our church has shared the full gospel in their own words to others.

TRUE HUMANITY

True Humanity, our second discipleship pathway essential, homes in on our life, identity, and purpose being connected personally to Jesus. It helps shape us into the likeness of Christ because it addresses the need to imitate Jesus; only through him do we live a life out of the growing knowledge of who God is and who we are meant to be as humans. Jesus informs us, transforms us completely, and loves us with his self-giving love.

We developed a tool that helps connect the true humanity essential ("I know who I am because I am personally connected to Jesus") to the mark of maturity ("They begin to not recognize themselves, saying, 'Before I used to ___, but now I find myself ___'") called "low planks." This practical tool helps us address sanctification, or inside-out transformation, and how this process has nothing to do with a self-help or self-improvement program but is about becoming an entirely new person being formed because of our new life in Jesus. We developed this tool to help move people from behavior modification to addressing the heart.

Table 5.3. True humanity tool: Low planks

Low planks: Deep heart work								
Purity	Integrity	Discipline	Faithful trust	Selflessness	Gentleness	Humility	Generosity	Other?
Lust	Dishonesty	Laziness	Fear	Selfishness	Anger/ resentment	Pride	Greed	

Using the simple chart above, the "low planks" tool helps disciples consider what parts of their lives are not fully imitating the heart of Jesus. For instance, if they are living more out of greed than generosity today, they would indicate it on the chart, and so on and so forth for each of the deep heart work elements. They would then break out into smaller pods of people to have a more intimate space of confession and conversation, and close with asking Jesus for help and the community to faithfully walk with them in their deep heart work.

Table 5.4. How to fill out low planks tool

Low planks: Deep heart work								
Purity	Integrity	Discipline	Faithful trust	Selflessness	Gentleness	Humility	Generosity	Other?
Lust	Dishonesty	Laziness	Fear	Selfishness	Anger/ resentment	Pride	Greed	

THICK COMMUNITY

Thick Community is our third discipleship pathway essential, because community is what Jesus was banking on to change the world and usher in his kingdom. As Christine Pohl notes, "The best testimony to the truth of the gospel is the quality of our life together. Jesus risked his reputation and the credibility of his story by tying them to how his followers live and care for one another in community. . . . Human beings were made for living in community, and it is in community that we flourish and become most fully human."[2] The truth of the full gospel and how we live as true humanity are tied closely to how we do life together.

One tool we use that helps to link the Thick Community essential ("I belong to God's unified, growing, and diverse family") to the mark of maturity ("They tell stories about how they are able to work well with and enjoy others who are different from them") is called "thin versus thick community."[3] In the moments when we experience the tension of wanting to move in opposite directions as a community—whether because of differing opinions, preferences, or relational conflict—we need to choose how to have love for one another. Think of a tug-of-war game: the thinness or thickness of the rope doesn't have any bearing on the game if it's about moving toward one another; the thickness of the rope matters only when we are moving away from one another. A piece of thread will not endure even one tug before it snaps in half, while a thick braided rope will stay together despite strong forces pulling in opposite directions.

If we live in a thin community, the bond will easily break as we move away from one another, but if we live in a thick community, the bond will stay strong despite these opposing forces. Jesus' way of doing life together—using community to show the world who he is—means fighting for a bond that will not easily break. This means asking ourselves these questions:

- When we are building relationships and conflict occurs, do we choose to be suspicious of the other person, or will we trust them because we are striving for a community of Jesus' love?

- When it comes to telling the truth and differences occur, do we choose to withhold information or our feelings from the other person, or will we be courageous and speak honestly with the grace and love that abounds in Jesus' community?

- When it comes to making peace and tension is present in the community, do we choose to breed thoughts and feelings of division, whether great or small, or will we invest in the other person and create environments of safe and freeing dialogue?

Table 5.5. Thick community tool

Element of community	Thin bond response	Thick bond response
Relationship building	Suspicion	Trust
Truth-telling	Hiding	Honesty
Peacemaking	Division	Dialogue

This tool equips the discipleship core (bounded set) to love and live in community in the way of Jesus. We have each disciple rate themself and one another in how they are doing in thick community using the scale provided (see table 5.6). It's a tool intended not for performance but for vulnerability.

Table 5.6. Thick community reflection scale tool

1–5	Thick community
	Relationship building: Trust versus suspicion When conflict or tension occurs, this person chooses to trust the other person instead of being suspicious of that person.
	Truth-telling: Honesty versus hiding When conflict or tension occurs, this person chooses to speak honestly with grace and love to address it instead of withholding information or feelings from that person.
	Peacemaking: Dialogue versus division When conflict or tension occurs, this person chooses to invest in the other person and create environments of safe and freeing dialogue instead of breeding divisive and resentful thoughts and feelings about the other person.
SCALE	
5: Exceptionally mature. A consistent way of life, such that if everyone in our community imitated this person, our whole community would flourish.	
4: Commendable. A strength in this person's life, where there is little need for improvement.	
3: Competent. Acceptable, reliable, capable in the *doing*, where there is still need for minor improvement (there is probably a head knowledge about the theme but a need for inner heart or motivation change).	
2: Growth needed. There's an awareness and acknowledgment of this needed growth, but it is a place of weakness, stagnation, or struggle.	
1: Poor. There's a lack of awareness or acknowledgment that spills over into our whole community that can block flourishing.	
N/A: Not applicable. Unable to reflect on this due to unobserved theme.	

Because a strong community matters to Jesus, disciples must learn to choose trust over suspicion, honesty over hiding, and dialogue over division over and over again. It was one of the last things Jesus told his closest friends, his disciples, before he laid down his life for us, and his kingdom is built upon us having love for one another (Jn 15:12-14).

HEART FOR THE ONE

Heart for the One, our fourth discipleship pathway essential, captures the heart and mission of Jesus. During his ministry on earth, Jesus time after time emphasized seeking two things: first, the kingdom of God, and second, that those far from him would come near (Lk 19:10), turning from darkness to light (Acts 26:18). If discipleship is about imitating Jesus, then we begin to love and seek the ones Jesus loves and seeks.

A tool that connects the Heart for the One essential ("I share with others God's heart of self-giving love") to the mark of maturity ("They tell us about people they are personally praying for and reaching out to") is called "five alive." The tool is simple and it goes like this:

1. Name five people in your life who don't know Jesus personally today.
2. Commit to praying every day that your "five alive" would become alive in Christ.
3. Commit to asking Jesus for opportunities to actively participate in helping your five alive to meet Jesus in a personal way.

The point of this tool is not to create a pressure to perform and "save" people—only the Holy Spirit transforms hearts—it is for every disciple to create a personal rhythm in their life that shares in God's heart for the one and to be transformed by his compassion and hope.

KINGDOM PARTNERSHIP

Finally, the fifth and last essential in our discipleship pathway is Kingdom Partnership. Most of us think of a kingdom as a geographic location like a nation or empire, but the more correct definition of the word "kingdom" is, as Dallas Willard puts it, "the range of effective will."[4] The kingdom of God refers to any space, place, or people where Jesus reigns and rules. It is where Jesus' word, thought, desire, will, and character have the first and final say. Lesslie Newbigin says:

> The question which has to be put to every local congregation is the question
> of whether it is a credible sign of God's reign in justice and mercy over the
> whole of life, whether it is an open fellowship whose concerns are as wide

as the concerns of humanity, whether it cares for its neighbors in a way which reflect and springs out of God's care for them, whether its common life is recognizable as a foretaste of the blessing which God intends for the whole human family.[5]

The question to our churches and communities is whether we are vibrant, life-giving partners in God's beautiful kingdom. Do wo participate in his reign of justice and mercy, of open fellowship that considers the concerns of everyone, of compelling compassion for our neighborhoods and communities, and of immense flourishing for the sake of the culture and world around us?

The tool that helps us match the Kingdom Partnership essential ("I actively participate in the life-giving reign of God") to the mark of maturity ("They can tell us why God has put them where they are in the world and the ways in which he is using them") is called "spaces, places, people." If a community of people were to live in the kingdom of God and partner with Jesus in it, we would begin to explore how the people, culture, and environments around us could be transformed. So what are the spaces, places, and people we come in contact with on the regular that God has already put us in? How would you fill out the chart in table 5.7?

Table 5.7. Kingdom partnership tool: Spaces, places, people

Spaces (Resources, hobbies, roles, etc.)	Places (Locations)	People (Relationships and networks)
Bank account/finances	Work	Family
Softball league	School	Coworkers
Parent-teacher association	Neighborhood	Friends
		Barista

If we as disciples are actively and intentionally participating in the kingdom of God, then by default, the spaces, places, and people in our lives will flourish and be transformed more and more into Jesus' kingdom of light, goodness, joy, generosity, peace, and self-giving love.

ESSENTIALS, TOOLS, AND MATURITY

The five essentials in our discipleship pathway (Full Gospel, True Humanity, Thick Community, Heart for the One, and Kingdom Partnership) are connected to marks of Christlike maturity in character, theology, wisdom, and missional living through a variety of tools. We know which tools work and which don't based on our clear marks of maturity, and we're flexible in changing the tools, but we stay faithful to the five essentials. In our church, we have three to five different tools for each essential, and the list keeps growing. Our list of tools grows for two main reasons: one, different tools are necessary for different discipleship cores, and two, new leaders develop their own tools for their discipleship cores and contribute to the collective toolbox.

When one of our leaders realized her discipleship core was wrestling with individual brokenness and sin, she camped on "act two" of the full gospel. She developed a tool that helped people identify the lie they were believing about God or themselves, and they took time to pray and read Scripture over one another to ground themselves firmly in Jesus as truth (Jn 14:6). The discipleship core became a people who not only recognized their own lies and one another's lies but reminded one another of the truth.

Another leader noticed that his discipleship core was extremely shy and had a tendency to hide from truth-telling. He needed them to grow in sharing with one another to deepen their Thick Community, so he started doing "thoughtful Thursdays" where everyone brought along a quote, a story, a song, or a Bible verse that captured their attention and showed what God might have been drawing their attention toward. By having a normal expected rhythm of sharing in this small way, the discipleship core grew into a group of people who shared their personal stories more deeply with one another.

Our discipleship pathway now has nearly fifty different tools, and all of our leaders have access to them. Their aim is to connect our five essentials to the marks of mature disciples. They are multiplying disciples who understand God's story, have a deep personal connection to Jesus, live in thick community, have a sincere heart for others, and who partner with Jesus in his expanding kingdom.

6

THE JOURNEY OF A DISCIPLESHIP PATHWAY

Some journeys take us far from home.
Some adventures lead us to our destiny.

C. S. LEWIS

It was just before the Passover Festival. Jesus knew
that the hour had come for him to leave this world
and go to the Father. Having loved his own who
were in the world, he loved them to the end.

JOHN 13:1

MY HUSBAND AND I HAVE THREE ADOLESCENTS, and one of our favorite activities is to go on a family bike ride together. Every time we go into our shed to pull each of the bicycles out, I have to look at a particular one that hasn't been used for a while, carefully leaning on the side of the wall. It's my husband's Quintana Roo. If you're an avid cyclist or have run the marathon circuits, you'll know what that is. It's a racing bike, and a really good one. In fact, my husband purchased this fancy racing bike because he had competed in a half Ironman called the Black Bear Triathlon in Pennsylvania. He swam 1.2 miles, biked 56 miles, and then transitioned right into running 13.1 miles. He came in fortieth place overall. And this was the first time he had competed in this event.

When my husband trained, he didn't just cover the distance for Black Bear; he put in twenty hours of swimming, cycling, and running a week for thirty weeks. He planned out when his practice runs would be, went to the YMCA before dawn to get his swims in before work, and spent weekends cycling miles upon miles. No one wakes up one morning and decides to compete in a Half Ironman; it takes development, proper gear, planning, and mastering the basics in order to compete. Every time I look at that Quintana Roo I think of the picture of my husband taken during the last leg of the race—he was in his running gear nearing the finish line, perspiration streaming, and a look of exhaustion in his frame, but the most memorable part was the bright, huge smile stretching from ear to ear. There was deep joy in the race.

Discipleship is no different.

No one wakes up one morning and decides to be a mature disciple of Jesus; it takes development, proper formation of both spiritual confidence and social competence,[1] practice (and a safe place to practice), and a community of people who are also imitating Jesus.

Often we think discipleship is experienced privately, conveniently, and organically. Experiencing discipleship privately means we do it on our own, perhaps through a book or some personal quiet time, and keep our learning and growing to ourselves. Our expectation then is that there will be no accountability, peer reflection, or mirroring helping us examine whether we are maturing into the likeness of Christ. Experiencing discipleship conveniently pertains to how easy or timely discipleship is. Our expectation is that discipleship fits our personality and calendar. If growing into the likeness of Jesus feels disruptive or challenging to my life, then it isn't for me. Experiencing discipleship organically creates an illusion that maturity happens haphazardly, without routine, rhythms, or resources. Our expectation is that discipleship doesn't necessarily need to be committed to a communal structure and pace.

The truth of the matter is that in Jesus' ministry, he engaged his disciples communally, with both challenge and intent. He was preparing them to be sent out, empowered by the Holy Spirit, "to Jerusalem, and in all Judea and Samaria, and to the ends of the earth" (Acts 1:8). Discipleship happens in community and requires commitment and intentional preparation, all of which produces people who are both spiritually confident and socially competent to love God, one another, and the culture and community around them.

The discipleship pathway is just that—helping those we lead and love become proficient in the essentials of what it means to be imitators of Christ. A discipleship pathway intentionally and clearly prepares people to experience deep joy in the journey of imitating Jesus for the sake of the world.

REMEMBER MATURITY

We have to keep in mind that the goal of discipleship and a discipleship pathway has nothing to do with completing an assignment or providing programming for increased head knowledge. The goal (and measure) of a discipleship pathway is how people are maturing into the likeness of Christ. And maturity is, in the simplest of terms, being transformed in Christlike character, theology, wisdom, and missional living. Mature disciples develop and grow in a new way of living—in tending to their inner person, engaging discipleship within an intentional community, and working together for the good of the neighborhood (or network) around them. The purpose of being equipped in five to eight basic essentials of a discipleship pathway is to become more mature. And mature disciples go and make mature disciples.

As leaders, we must become crystal clear about what our discipleship pathway is and how it's enfolded in the life and structure of our churches and communities.

BUILDING THE JOURNEY

The following are contours to consider in shaping and building your discipleship pathway. The journey isn't just about an outline; it's about the form and function of an object. How the light hits it, where its shadows and open spaces are, what impression and appearance it gives when you experience it from one angle to another. A powerful and compassionate framework is meaningful, formational, communal, renewing, and rhythmic with the goal and fruit of maturity in mind.

Table 6.1. Building the discipleship pathway journey

Journey of a discipleship pathway	
Meaningful	Relevant content and tools for maturity
Formational	Practice-based content and tools for practicing maturity
Communal	Setting and safety for every disciple to participate
Renewal	Formation tied to local mission in the neighborhood (or network)
Rhythmic	Cyclic pattern of maturing as disciples and making disciples

Meaningful. Praxis is deeply connected to content and the means by which content is not just delivered but lived out. Content and tools that are tied to the praxis of discipleship are vital to equip people in the way of Christ for the renewal of the culture and community around them. Content has to do with the five to eight essentials of your discipleship pathway, and the tools are how you want to equip disciples to grow into maturity.

- What content is in your discipleship pathway?
- What tools do you want disciples to become proficient in?
- How will you assemble the material, both content and tools for praxis, into the discipleship pathway?

The meaningful content in our discipleship pathway is found in the five essentials that are meaningful to our locally rooted setting:

- Full Gospel: Understanding and participating in God's story
- True Humanity: Understanding and participating in who we really are in Christ
- Thick Community: Understanding and participating in how we live together
- Heart for the One: Understanding and participating in God's heart of self-giving love
- Kingdom Partnership: Understanding and participating in how the kingdom of God works

Each of these five essentials in our local church keeps the marks of maturity in mind.

When I was working with a church in Portland, the meaningful essentials they were working on came from their vision for their multicultural and multigenerational church sitting at the heart of a racially contentious part of the city. Their vision statement was "Creating a Diverse Community of Justice for Portland." As we started looking at what essentials would be meaningful for their community, we landed on five: Diversity, Community, Justice, Love, and Portland Neighborhood.

The tools that the leadership wanted their church to be proficient in included how to embrace and seek out diversity in ethnicity, age, gender, and socioeconomics; how to be an active community member not just in church life but in the life of the neighborhood; how to act justly and love mercy for their neighborhood as God does (Mic 6:8); how to immerse themselves in the identity of God's love for them and for one another (Jn 13: 34); and how to seek the peace of Portland (Jer 29:7).

Formational. A discipleship pathway is not about downloading information to people and hoping that this will equate to maturity. Imitating Jesus is about formation, reformation, and transformation of the whole person; therefore a discipleship pathway must consider how the content and the practice of the content shape the heart, mind, soul, and might for missional living.

- How does your discipleship pathway shape the whole person?
- How will your discipleship pathway include both physical and embodied practices?
- What tool or framework will you use to exercise hearts, minds, souls, and might for missional living?

Each of the five essentials in our church body's discipleship pathway is formative beyond mere information. We design the essentials not just to form our minds but to be experienced and practiced.

Full Gospel is not only about knowing about God's story; praxis comes in encountering God's invitation to be an active part of his story. We experience what it means to be good and broken at the same time.

True Humanity is not only about understanding how Jesus defines what it means to be both truly human and God's image-bearer, but we practice asking the Father, "What do you think of me?" We ask the Son, "How do you feel about me?" And we ask the Holy Spirit, "What would you like me to do?"

Thick Community is not only learning about the diversity of the body of Christ but being equipped to engage practically in conflict resolution and seeking and extending forgiveness within our community.

Heart for the One is not just reading about the parable of the lost coin but actively participating in the lives of the people God is calling us to love and contend for daily.

And finally, Kingdom Partnership is not just knowing about how one day Jesus will return and we're just sitting on a golden access pass to heaven, but his here-and-now invitation for us to participate in the flourishing and renewal of everyone and everything around us.

For the multicultural, multiethnic church I worked with in Portland, their discipleship pathway became formational through the embedding of three key questions at every discipleship core gathering. After a time of learning together, they answered the following questions that connected their learning to praxis:

- How does Jesus address ____?
- How do I personally address ___?
- How do we as a community address ___?

For instance, if they were being equipped in an essential around justice, they would take time to dialogue and mutually grow from considering how Jesus addresses justice, how each of them addresses (or does not address) justice, and how their community ought to address justice issues in their own neighborhood.

Table 6.2. Example of a discipleship pathway: Portland, Oregon

Essential	Tool	Mark of Maturity
Diversity	• How does Jesus address diversity? • How do I personally address (or not address) diversity? • How do we as a community address (or not address) diversity?	They begin to journey alongside others who are different from them in race, age, gender, and socioeconomics.
Community	• How does Jesus address community? • How do I personally address (or not address) community? • How do we as a community address (or not address) community?	They begin to share stories about friendships and doing life with those in the church and neighborhood community outside of Sunday worship gatherings.

Table 6.2. (continued)

Essential	Tool	Mark of Maturity
Justice	• How does Jesus address justice? • How do I personally address (or not address) justice? • How do we as a community address (or not address) justice?	• They begin to ask questions around justice and injustice issues in their lives and the lives of others. • They begin to share stories of understanding what mercy looks like in the face of justice and injustice.
Love	• How does Jesus address love? • How do I personally address (or not address) love? • How do we as a community address (or not address) love?	• They share stories of being loved and known by God and being loved and known by others. • They share stories of loving and knowing others.
Neighborhood	• How does Jesus address our neighborhood? • How do I personally address (or not address) our neighborhood? • How do we as a community address (or not address) our neighborhood?	• They begin to ask questions about what God is doing in the city and neighborhood. • They know how to participate in God's work in the city and neighborhood.

Communal. In building a discipleship pathway that both informs and immerses us in the missional way of Jesus, we must also construct safe spaces where relationship will be cultivated. Discipleship never takes place apart from community—a family of people who are out to mature into the likeness of Christ together. Cultivating practices of belonging and safety also creates holy places that resist environments of shame, abdication, and performance.

- How do you plan relational safety? Around a regular meal?
- Where will you meet that communicates warmth and being able to let one's guard down?
- How will you give space for people to share feelings of inadequacy, fear, or struggle?

Our discipleship pathway is always experienced in sitting around a dinner together. Our biweekly discipleship core (bounded set) meets every other week around a table, where we begin with one person leading us in Communion and having intentional conversation about how we have seen God moving in, through, and around us, or how it's been difficult to see the movement of God.

The first hour is dedicated to eating a meal together, sharing, and re-connecting. The next twenty minutes is reserved for equipping in one of the five essentials in our discipleship pathway, and the rest of the two-hour total time frame has us dividing up into smaller pods of three to four people to discuss what resonated with us, what was still confusing, and what feels like conflict in us as we seek to mature into the likeness of Christ individually and as a committed community. Even in the in-between times we are intentionally paired up so we can have further conversation about the discipleship pathway essential or how we lived the content out in our personal rhythm.

The Portland church focuses on making their discipleship pathway communal by setting it biweekly around a meal. At dinner, they set the stage for safety and growth by asking in groups of two to three, "Since the last time we've been together, what is God doing in you, through you, and around you? What might be hindering you from seeing God at work?" It quickly establishes a culture of both vulnerability and awareness, with lots of room for not being aware of what God is doing in you, through you, and around you.

Renewing. Jesus was not about forming a large crowd around an institution. He was about doing life deeply with his disciples and equipping them so the movement would grow like wildfire from deep relationship, imitation, and practice. And deep relationship, imitation, and praxis of discipleship happens within a community of people who are, one, on mission together and, two, discipling others. Discipleship must be tied to mission, and mission is what makes discipleship a movement. Movement (and not just an institution) happens when people experience the real-life, real-time work of intentionally building, laboring over, and loving an active community and the neighborhood (or network) it engages with.

- How will you make sure your discipleship pathway is tied to a missional community?
- How do you identify those who will be discipled within a missional community?
- How will you equip those you're discipling to disciple others within a missional community?

Every multiplied missional community (centered set) in our church is tethered to a discipleship core (bounded set) that is moving through a discipleship pathway together. We have a loose criteria of what clearly makes a community a missional community:

- The leader or leaders have completed or will complete a discipleship pathway.
- A missional space (co-mission, purpose, work of renewal) has been identified and already engaged in the last six months.
- The leaders will not be leading on their own—there is clear intent or process to intentionally connect with others who are committed to the emerging discipleship core and to the identified space of mission in their community.

Every new missional community leader is deeply equipped in the discipleship pathway and continues to be strongly supported as they practice discipling others. There's always encouragement to redesign a more unique and specific portrait of the tools of discipleship in order to better engage and equip their own discipleship core. And they do this while holding on to the clarity of our five essentials of discipleship and marks of maturity.

The church in Portland kept their first discipleship core tied to renewal by having the group lead a quarterly neighborhood event such as a neighborhood block party for Juneteenth or supporting a local Black businesswoman. In the second year of their journey, they multiplied into three discipleship cores in three different parts of the neighborhood, with new leaders leading a diverse group of people through the discipleship pathway.

Rhythmic. A discipleship pathway is not a program—it's a missional lifestyle that forms the heartbeat of your church and community. It's how you measure the pulse and vibrancy of your people and their engagement in community and mission together. It waxes and wanes depending on the life of your church and community, particularly in receiving and sending people out. While the essentials and marks of maturity stay the same, how you cultivate formation, relationship, and movement are flexible given the life of the church, but discipleship is never pushed aside. Discipleship is the center that the life of the church and community orients around.

- How long is your discipleship pathway? Six months, nine months, twelve months? Is it feasible to go through the entire pathway in that time?
- How is one held accountable to their commitment?
- What happens at the end of the cycle?

In my church, the cycle of discipleship varies depending on the particular missional community (centered set). We have a discipleship pathway that a community can cycle through in six, twelve, or eighteen months, depending on the needs of that particular discipleship core (bounded set). People communicate their commitment by having either one-on-one or group conversations discussing clearly what commitment to a bounded set will entail. We often do this through an annual Vision Day that allows those who want to participate in a discipleship core in the coming season to make a clear commitment.

At the end of the cycle, disciples either go on to start their own missional community tethered to their own discipleship core or team up in leadership to help lead an existing missional community that's tethered to an incoming new group of people committing to a new discipleship core. Sometimes the discipleship core commits to continuing another cycle (six or twelve months) together in order to grow in specific aspects of the discipleship pathway together, often due to increasing leadership or praxis in mission.

The Portland church journeys through their rhythm in a twelve-month cycle, meeting twice a month as shown in table 6.3.

Table 6.3. Example of a discipleship pathway rhythm: Portland, Oregon

Month	Discipleship pathway rhythm
January	Set the big picture
	Set the discipleship rhythm
February	Diversity
	Diversity
March	Diversity
	Diversity—practice into the neighborhood
April	Community
	Community

Table 6.3. (continued)

Month	Discipleship pathway rhythm
May	Community
	Community—practice into the neighborhood
June	Justice
	Justice
July	Justice
	Justice—practice into the neighborhood
August	Love
	Love
September	Love
	Love—practice into the neighborhood
October	Neighborhood
	Neighborhood
November	Neighborhood
	Neighborhood—practice into the neighborhood
December	Celebration—start inviting next discipleship core
	Celebration—start inviting next discipleship core

At the end of the calendar year, as they celebrate, they also start to invite others from their church and neighborhood into a multiplied discipleship core starting the following year. Because they have been maturing together in the likeness of Jesus, the original discipleship core divides into three different groups the following year, helping to lead a new discipleship core. With three new discipleship cores, each shares the rhythm of leading the at-large church into the neighborhood quarterly.

JOURNEY INTO MULTIPLICATION

What would happen to our churches and communities if the time, effort, and intent we as leaders pour into establishing a public worship service was geared toward shaping and (re)structuring our churches to make discipleship central? What would happen if we as leaders thoughtfully and compassionately invested ourselves in making discipleship central by developing a discipleship pathway that is meaningful, formational, communal, renewing, and rhythmic for our people? We would move from entertaining and trying to persuade spectators to leading mature disciples who reflect to the community, culture, and world around them the beauty, mercy, joy, and justice of Jesus. We would be intentionally and actively doing life with mature disciples who are making mature disciples.

Haku is a young Hawaiian man who started coming to our Open Spaces weekly community dinner the first year. He enjoyed sitting around a table of six to eight people, sharing a meal and sharing a story, each week. As he started to connect more with the disciples in our community, in the second year he started asking questions around faith and Jesus. He participated in a series of conversations our church hosts annually called Jesus Conversations where we have an open dialogue about Jesus in someone's backyard around a fire pit. He said yes to Jesus and joined a discipleship core the following year. He participated in a discipleship pathway, journeying with other disciples through the essentials of understanding God's story, being personally connected to Jesus, being a part of a thick community, having a heart for the one, and partnering with God in his kingdom work. The following year he helped lead a new discipleship core, coteaching and equipping them through the discipleship pathway, growing personally not just in his teaching gift but also relearning the essentials in a deeper way.

Haku is now going to be sent out to start a new missional community altogether, as he has a heart for the local youth in Hawaii. Haku is on a journey to being a mature disciple who is making more mature disciples.

PART 3

UNDERLYING ASSUMPTIONS OF DISCIPLESHIP

When the church becomes an end in itself, it ends.

ROBBY GALLATY

7

DISCIPLESHIP REQUIRES TRANSFORMATION

*Every successful social movement in this country's
history has used disruption as a strategy to fight for
social change. Whether it was the Boston Tea Party
to the sit-ins at lunch counters throughout the South,
no changes has been won without disruptive action.*

ALICIA GARZA

*As Jesus walked beside the Sea of Galilee, he saw
Simon and his brother Andrew casting a net into the
lake, for they were fishermen. "Come, follow me,"
Jesus said, "and I will send you out to fish for people."
At once they left their nets and followed him.*

MARK 1:16-18

WE HAD JUST ARRIVED WITH OUR BABY BOY for the weekend visiting my in-laws. My husband, Steve, and I, then nervous new parents, had just driven four hours after work and sat in bumper-to-bumper traffic on the I-95 with our fifteen-month-old. All we wanted to do was get him down for bed. We exchanged greetings with Steve's parents, who were ecstatic to host us for the weekend, and went right to work getting our son down for the night.

It was a source of pride and joy for us that we had an angel of a baby who slept peacefully through the night without difficulty. It typically took us all of five minutes to do a bedtime routine and count him as down for the night. It was like a party trick when friends were over; they would expect the bedtime-designated parent to be away for hours putting the baby to bed, and invariably their jaws would drop when we returned within minutes. This night would be no different. I took our son upstairs to put him down in his crib for the night. Same routine, same bedtime stories, same goodnight.

Except it wasn't the same. As soon as I laid him in his crib, he pulled himself right back up and started to fuss. No sooner had I laid him back down but he popped back up and started to cry. And cry. And cry. After a while I just left him to cry and went to join the family. I was confused and frustrated—what was wrong with him? He'd never behaved this way before! I reported that the baby was going to cry for a while and left it at that. My husband said he would give it a try, even though I warned him it wouldn't be worth the effort. But then, ten minutes later, Steve came back down and there was no crying.

"What did you do?" I asked him, suspiciously.

"Oh, I held him for a bit and showed him around my old bedroom. I whispered to him, 'I know change is hard, buddy, but we can get through it together.'"

Steve is right: change is hard.

In my community, change reared its ugly head at a pace that was hard to handle. Because we started with a discipleship core and not a public worship service, it was hard from the get-go. We didn't have the familiar rhythm of corporate worship and preaching. When we launched our first missional community, a weekly community dinner, and were expected to invite our friends, coworkers, neighbors, and family who did not know Jesus on a weekly basis, it was hard. Not having a worship service to draw a crowd and having to rely on personal invitation was hard.

It was hard when the discipleship pathway revealed that many of us didn't know what the gospel was. It was hard when the discipleship pathway began to expose the sin of envy in our community. It was hard when the discipleship pathway began to highlight that some of us didn't have non-Christian friendships or that we didn't really know our neighbors.

It was hard when multiplication was about to happen and some people were ready for it and others were not. It was hard when multiplication did happen and new leaders started to emerge; some people from the initial discipleship core had a hard time embracing new people and new roles. Our church is now going through yet another change: we are in the process of transitioning from one lead pastor (me) to three co-lead pastors.

Change is hard.

When it comes to deeply and intentionally discipling a group of people to imitate Jesus by being committed to one another as a sent community in order to be on mission together, growth invariably happens. And growth, which often presents itself as change, is hard.

GROWTH AND CHANGE GO HAND IN HAND

In Matthew 13:31-32 we read, "He told them another parable: 'The kingdom of heaven is like a mustard seed, which a man took and planted in his field. Though it is the smallest of all seeds, yet when it grows, it is the largest of garden plants and becomes a tree, so that the birds come and perch in its branches.'"

Growth is a natural element of how the kingdom of God functions. The mustard seed grows to be the largest plant in the garden and provides flourishing for everything and everyone around it. But, as Jesus describes in this parable, the kingdom of God does not grow by staying stagnant in its initial form. The tiniest of all the seeds grows to become what we would not originally foresee: the largest of plants that brings rest, safety, and abundance to its surrounding environment. With growth, the mustard seed changes to be something it wasn't before. But growth always means change. And change is hard.

Anticipating growth, and therefore anticipating change, is pivotal for deeply discipling people to become a sent community on mission together. Change seems disruptive, inconsistent, and even noncommittal and disloyal at times; most people would resonate with the idea that change makes us uncomfortable because it seems untrustworthy. When we as leaders want to engage the people we lead and love into a process of change and growth, we are often met with resistance; the effort of contending against that resistance requires immense effort. It's easy to label people who are not willing to accept change with unflattering descriptions. Stubborn. Unimaginative. Stuck in their ways. But the truth is that people often resist change for two reasons: one, they believe they will lose something of value that is worth protecting, or, two, they fear they will be thrown to the wayside because they won't be able to fully participate and adapt to the change.

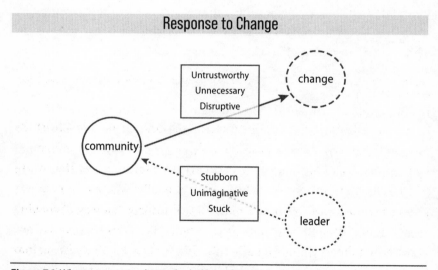

Figure 7.1. What response to change looks like at first glance

Instead of seeing change as the enemy and thereby inhibiting growth, we can continue to look to the parable of the mustard seed. The way we know change is leading to growth that depicts the kingdom of God is to look at what the change is providing for its surroundings. If change is allowing for the kind of growth that establishes rest, beauty, goodness, abundance, righteousness, partnership, and wholeness that only God's faithful presence can bring about, then that's the kind of change we're looking for. It's the kind of change that helps us experience the natural element of growth found in the kingdom of God.

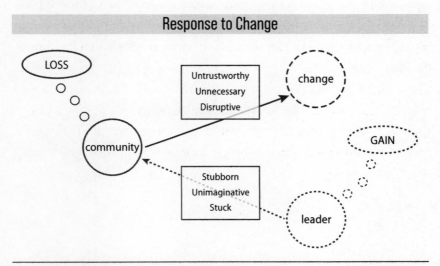

Figure 7.2. The leader first considers gain as a response to change while the community often first considers loss as a response to change

For years I have been discipling others into the likeness of Christ. By the time I had come into a position of full-time covocational ministry, I had already discipled fifty people in one-on-one settings over the course of a decade. That's on average of five people annually! Discipleship was just part of my normal. Over time I realized that my normal way of shaping and forming disciples had huge gaps. The biggest was that while they experienced the value of being discipled, they weren't actively living into the greater value of making disciples. In order for growth to happen, I needed to make a change.

Years later I gathered a group of twenty-four men and women in our community to deeply and intentionally disciple them in a way where they would learn to model discipleship—that is, they would begin to disciple others. Instead of doing my normal one-on-one personalized discipleship, I started doing group discipleship, where the intent was explicitly becoming fully equipped to make more disciples. Unbeknownst to me, in just six months' time, the twenty-four disciples quickly became disciples who were making more disciples. In fact, over a hundred individuals in our community were being deeply and intentionally discipled in both one-on-one and group settings within six months. When I looked back to what I had accomplished alone in a decade, I realized this change brought about a growth that doubled my meager efforts in a fraction of the time.

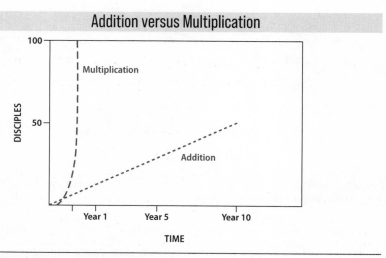

Figure 7.3. Addition versus multiplication in discipleship

Growth requires change. And change is hard. If we're honest with ourselves as leaders, the idea of launching communities on mission and deeply and intentionally discipling a group of people to imitate Jesus *instead of* launching a weekly Sunday service is a new concept for most of us. The idea of multiplying disciples who are committed to one another and committed to the real-life locally rooted community around them for the sake of a neighborhood or social network seems like a huge change. Too often, while the growth aspect is desirable, the change that comes with it seems daunting.

- Where do we start?
- How do we confront the need to change?

- What do we need to do?

- Who do we address?

- How do we get people on board for growth?

- How can we compassionately engage with them given people's general resistance to change?

- What value are people are protecting and guarding?

- How are people feeling left out or ill-equipped to participate in the change?

Even within multiplied missional communities, the change that comes with growth is difficult to navigate. How do we, then, approach change in the midst of growth in order to love and lead our congregations and communities wisely?

TRADITIONAL, TRANSITIONAL, TRANSFORMATIONAL

In order to know how to approach change, we need to know that there are different responses to change. Our motivation for change, our willingness to change, and how we think about change really matter. When we as leaders want to hold on to tradition, we will only make incremental improvements. When we want to straddle both the next level of change and safety, then we will make changes through transitions. But change that is transformational involves a vision for a new way of living within a new infrastructure that requires a significant breakthrough in mindset in order to pursue new opportunities.[1]

While not everything requires a transformational response, I submit that making discipleship central to the life of our churches and communities requires transformational change.

Because the nature of growth requires change, the first thing to address as leaders is how we go about the change that comes with participating in the kingdom of God. Deconstructing how change takes place shows us there are three ways of approaching and engaging with change: traditional, transitional, and transformational.

Most of us in church leadership find that our communities in need of change and growth are often stuck in the *traditional* approach to change. Our thoughts are focused on incremental improvements, whether in skills or practices, to improve our current model. Our leadership revolves around the ever-appealing need for comfort and complacency. The motivation for change is to keep the framework, method, and model intact while changing only the aspects that bring about a better, faster, or more cost-effective result. With incremental improvement, the response to change is safely manageable and controlled, often requiring leadership only to improve on a skill, practice, or performance. It requires individual improvement versus a systematic change. An example of traditional change to making discipleship central is including more discipleship topics in our sermon series or offering a Sunday school session on discipleship. It doesn't change anything about the current model of church.

Others of us live in the *transitional* approach to change, where we design and implement a plan to fix a problem in our current model,

Table 7.1. Approaches to change

Three types of change			
	Traditional	**Transitional**	**Transformational**
Motivation for change	Make our current model better, faster, or cheaper	Fix a problem in current model	Vision changes our current model
Degree of change	Incremental improvements of current model	Transition current model from old version (A) to new version (B)	New and necessary model
Thoughts around change	Current model works, just need some improvements	Current model works, just need to fix management or strategy	Current model is not working; need a new model
Goal of change	Improvement on current model	Complete new plan or project for current model	Committed to vision over current model
Leadership requirement for change	Improvement of skills, practices, or performance	Ability to control a process and manage, assign, direct projects	Commitment to new thinking, learning, and modeling; courage
Adapted from Marcia Daszko and Sheila Sheinberg, "Survival Is Optional: Only Leaders with New Knowledge Can Pivot, Disrupt, & Lead a Transformation," LinkedIn, October 18, 2021, www.linkedin.com/pulse/survival-optional-only-leaders-new-knowledge-can-pivot-marcia-daszko.			

whether through an alteration in managing people or strategic planning to get from version A to version B. Our leadership revolves around the comfort in certainty. While the change seems large, it is addressing only an aspect of the current model. The "fix" involves experimenting with a new type of management or strategic planning framework that becomes project- and task-oriented. Transitional change often requires the leadership to focus on their ability to control a process or better manage a plan or project. It requires confined task-based pivots versus a grounding in a bigger vision. An example of transitional change to making discipleship central is hiring a discipleship pastor or getting a new discipleship curriculum for small groups. It replaces old management (people) or strategy (plan/project) without changing the current model of church.

A *transformational* approach to change involves an invitation to radical shifts in thinking and living, at times considering a whole system change, in order to stay committed to the vision at hand over the current model we use. The vision motivates the need for change, not the current model (structures, methods, plans, etc.). The degree of change is new but necessary and the response to change allows for leaders to consider the whole system in light of the overarching vision. It requires leadership to be committed to new thinking, learning, and relearning in order to constantly tether the current structure and system to the vision. And this way of leading in a transformational way takes courage.

Making discipleship central requires a radical vision to grow and change. It requires vision to multiply communities on mission together and deeply and intentionally disciple a group of people to imitate Jesus. It requires vision to invite disciples to be committed to one another as a sent community on mission together *over* executing Sunday worship services. It requires a revolutionary approach to multiply followers of Jesus who are living in community together for the sake of their collective neighbors instead of living out a privatized Christianity. It requires a kingdom vision to multiply disciples who are participating in making disciples in lieu of being comfortable spectators at an event.

In order to be motivated by a radical vision, we need to be anchored in God's love, and, with humility, understand how transformational approach to change works.

TRANSFORMATIONAL APPROACH TO CHANGE

Discipleship is at the heart of transformation, and discipleship simply means imitating Christ. Therefore, if imitation of Christ and discipleship are at the center of what we want to multiply, then our churches and communities will need to change. The need to change comes from reconsidering our current models, systems, and practices in ways that will intentionally transform our communities to become people who embody a radical faith, hope, and love (1 Cor 13:13). They will be communities living wholeheartedly and intentionally to be sent into the world for the sake of the world. But if we forsake our most basic task of making a community of disciples who are on mission together, then our churches and communities will be limited.

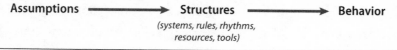

Figure 7.4. Transformational approach to change using change theory

A transformational approach to change helps us see what we may be missing. It provides a way for us as leaders to have the courage not just to incrementally improve or make a new plan for our current models of leading our churches but to engage in a new model to lead our communities into mission together. Popularized in the early 1990s through Carol Weiss's work in development and sociology, change theory gives us a glimpse into how the transformational approach works. The framework involves assessing and engaging assumptions, structures, and behaviors.[2]

- Assumptions are any of our current leadership and community's beliefs, habits, traditions, patterns, and paradigms held as valuable to support and live into a given framework. Assumptions are the why of what we do.

- Structures are any policies, procedures, systems, rhythms, resources, and tools that are built in order for the assumptions to be implemented. Structures are the "how" of what we do.

- Behavior is current practice, real-life activity, action, participation, language, common vocabulary, culture, and what the majority of people perceive as the norm. Behavior is the "what" in what we do.

In essence, what we assume drives structure, which provides an environment for specific behavior. At the heart of transformational change is both assessing and challenging our assumptions because assumptions critically drive structure, which produces behavior.

As a way to see what kind of change is necessary, we must first look at what behaviors exist in our congregation. For instance, we could ask this question: What does the behavior of my church and community say about what is important about being a disciple of Jesus?

For most of our communities, the primary behavior of our members is limited to attending Sunday service. Depending on the denominational tradition, they sing some worship songs together, listen to a sermon, and then make some heartfelt greetings before retreating back to their own private lives. Given the behavior, discipleship at best means church attendance.

The next piece to address is structures (the systems, rules, rhythms, resources, and tools) within our congregation that support the behavior. The question to consider is: What structures are in place that support that behavior in our church?

Table 7.2. Questions for transformation

Behavior	Structure	Assumption
What does the behavior of our church/community say about being a disciple?	What structures are in place that support that behavior in our church?	What underlying assumptions support this existing structure that produces this behavior?

Again, using the same example, we can see that the behavior of church attendance is dictated by the structure that is in place. Most of our leadership, resources, tools, rhythms, efforts, personnel, and focus are allocated to running a successful Sunday worship gathering. And where there's structure, behavior follows close behind.

We then turn to looking at what our underlying assumptions are, given both behavior and structure. Then the question to ask is: What underlying assumptions do we have to support this existing structure that produces this behavior?

In our example, some underlying assumptions that drive our structures, evidenced by behavior, are:

- Discipleship is measured by church attendance.
- Church is defined by gathering at a Sunday service.
- The leadership's role is to provide a successful Sunday service.

Invariably, this paints a picture that the most important thing to a disciple of Jesus is how they contribute to the church, which is defined by building the Sunday service, highlighting the teaching pastor, and labeling disciples as those who show up on Sundays. At best, mission is a once-in-a-while side event and Christian community means a self-contained good Bible study. Assumptions drive structures (including policies, procedures, systems, scheduling, training, etc.), which drive behavior.

While there is a sincere beauty in corporate worship services, we can recognize that making Sunday worship central to our church is not the radical vision of making discipleship central to our church. Having Sunday worship services be the keynote of our churches will not actively and intentionally make disciples who make more disciples.

RADICAL VISION FOR CHANGE

When we courageously examine our current model of discipleship and clearly see a narrative based on current behaviors dictated by current structures, we begin to see what our underlying assumptions are. If we're not satisfied with these assumptions, then we move into a practice that begins to help us change with wisdom. Identifying underlying assumptions helps us have an awareness of the need for transformation. Awareness then helps us to revisit the vision.

Awareness ——→ Vision ——→ Learning ——→ Action

Figure 7.5. Process for transformation moves from the leader growing in awareness for the need for change, revisiting their vision, identifying what they need to learn and relearn, and cultivating safe environments to practice change

For instance, following the same example, as we become aware of the fact that we're not really making disciples of Jesus by focusing on a weekly Sunday worship service, we are drawn back to the radical vision of Jesus' kingdom. Our vision is for our church to become disciples of Jesus who are committed to one another and to the community around us by multiplying imitators of Jesus who are sent as a community on mission together. Most churches' vision statements can be boiled down to "Love God, love people."

Revisiting the revolutionary vision helps us gain clarity on our marks of maturity, such as imagining together what kind of behaviors we would want in our congregation and what structures need to be changed in order for that to happen. If a behavior we imagine is that people are discipling others, then we need a structure that supports everyone being equipped in a discipleship pathway in order to make more disciples. The new underlying assumption is that the Great Commission is for everyone, not just some. If a behavior we imagine is that groups of people are being sent out on mission together in their shared neighborhoods, then we need a structure that supports missional communities to be a high value. The new underlying assumption is that multiplication of disciples is not happening in Sunday services; it's happening in the neighborhoods and in communities.

With clarity in vision, we move toward humble, flexible learning, which in turn shapes more learning. It is the type of learning where we are equipped in an environment of learning by doing. Learning the same concept in different locations enhances our learning; learning by teaching sharpens our learning; learning through trial and error emboldens our learning; learning through the fivefold gifts represented in the body widens our learning.

Finally, radical vision that is attached to humble and flexible learning leads to action, because knowledge without action is merely the accumulation of trivia. Action is the application of new learning, and applying what we learn leads to new living. Application of learning allows for new leaders to model discipleship and a community that actively lives into keeping discipleship central.

Table 7.3. Process for transformation to center discipleship

Awareness	Vision	Learning	Action
Examines our current behavior, structures, and assumptions	Revisits how our current vision aligns with the radical vision of Jesus	Clarity in vision leads to humble and flexible learning	Application of new learning leads to new living
Identifies our underlying assumptions	Examines what discipleship is and how central it is in our community	Learning by doing Learning in different environments Learning by teaching Learning through the fivefold gifts	Leads to new leaders who are modeling discipleship
Leads to revisiting the radical vision of Jesus	Considers the clear marks that show discipleship is central in our community	Learning via a variety of ways leads to practice in real life	Leads to a community that keeps discipleship central
	Leads to identifying what new learning is required for discipleship to be central		Leads to behavior that clearly marks the centrality of discipleship

BEING SENT REQUIRES TRANSFORMATION

As we courageously assess our own congregations and do a truthful dive into behaviors, structures, and underlying assumptions residing within our communities, leadership, and ourselves, we are invited to lead and love those God has given us into a vision that is intended for our goodness and the goodness of our neighborhoods and social networks. Making discipleship central in our churches and communities allows for the natural and inevitable element of growth that is a part of the kingdom of God. Making discipleship central allows for the people we lead and love to become a sent community who are on mission together for the sake of the locally rooted real-life community around them. Making discipleship central, with our identity and motivation anchored in the unending love of a missional God who sends us as communities on mission together, requires transformation.

In my community, we multiplied into three missional communities after the first year. The change brought an uncomfortable feeling for many of us. While going through a discipleship pathway together, two people began noticing more acutely the ways God was working and calling them to mission in their own neighborhood and network. Melissa began to identify her condominium as a clear neighborhood where she could replicate a regular community dinner and began to intentionally know and pray for her neighbors. Kelci was growing in her own passion for the elderly and narrowing it to one block of the city where there were three low-income senior living facilities. Our church needed to prepare to send Melissa and Kelci out, but this was going to require change. It requires change to rethink structure, leadership criteria, and plans for growth. This situation challenged those who weren't ready to be sent out; it challenged those who didn't want Melissa or Kelci to leave; it challenged Melissa and Kelci to step into leadership.

After six months of conversations, discernment, trial and error, and prayer, our community developed a framework that continues to exist today as we consider multiplication. One, we became a community that anticipates multiplication of missional communities every year and we include it in our annual budget. Two, we set clear criteria to become a multiplied missional community:

1. The leader must journey through a discipleship pathway.
2. The leader must identify a space of mission (neighborhood or network) and try out cultivating community for six months.
3. The leader must have a plan for establishing a discipleship core.

Because of these simple clarifications, Melissa and Kelci are not the only ones who have multiplied into a missional community. We have been multiplying missional communities every year since the start.

Transformation happens through the careful and humble work of intentionally growing in awareness, revisiting and realigning ourselves to Jesus' radical vision, learning practically with flexibility and humility, and participating in action by living on mission as a community. Transformation happens through awareness, vision, learning, and action. Transformation involves stretching and supporting people, as Steve did with our son, amid change. And the truth of the matter is that transformation is the work of the Holy Spirit who is residing inside of us, sending us, and already at work in the communities, neighborhoods, and social networks around us. The kingdom of God is growing, God is on the move, and movement happens through transformation.

8

UNMASKING OUR DISCIPLESHIP ASSUMPTIONS

If you always do what you've always done, then
you get what you've always gotten.

JESSIE POTTER

[Jesus] told them, "The secret of the kingdom
of God has been given to you. But to those on
the outside everything is said in parables."

MARK 4:11

IN MEDICAL SCHOOL, I found one of my classmates to be ridiculous. While I would try to beat rush hour traffic in Philadelphia to make it to my eight a.m. anatomy lectures on time, wearing a suitable yet comfortable outfit of button-down shirt, slacks, and flats for maximum support during the mad rush out of lecture hall to change into scrubs and get to the cadaver lab, this student took a different approach. She came in all dolled up, big hair, long acrylic nails, makeup precisioned on, clothes that pushed the boundaries of professionalism, and, worst of all, those heels. High heels. High heels that click-click-clicked all across the lecture hall and click-click-clicked to the locker rooms. They even click-click-clicked into the cadaver lab. Ridiculous. What was she thinking wearing such unreasonable, unnecessary foot apparel in medical school? Our dissection work and regurgitation of *Grey's Anatomy* was going to fuel our success, not our discretion for fashion. She was so ridiculous that I avoided her, and I was thankful when I wasn't put into her anatomy group.

Fast-forward a few years later, and I'm now in a clinic taking patients of my own for the first time. I'm in my button-down shirt, slacks, and flats for maximum support and comfort, and in comes that familiar click-click-click. I was face-to-face with my new patient: the one I found so ridiculous. She'd come to see me because her feet were so malformed and overarched that they caused her pain on a daily basis. In fact, the only way she could cope with the pain was to wear high-heeled shoes that supported her naturally overarched feet.

"Dr. Strawser, can you help me?"

My underlying assumption was that this woman was ridiculous because of her choice in footwear, and my underlying assumption was dead wrong.

The only way my dead-wrong assumption was going to be unmasked was for me to have to diagnose why she had to wear high heels on the daily. Not because of her vanity but because of her pain. Not because of her attention to fashion trends but because of her congenital pes cavus.

My underlying assumption about discipleship was also dead wrong when I thought discipleship happened best in one-on-one settings.

For the first half of my ministry, I only participated in one-on-one discipleship: it allowed me to go in-depth with the person, maintain undivided attention to all their questions, and tailor-fit the discipleship process to the individual. The problem I kept facing with this approach was threefold. One, it modeled a type of discipleship where you had to be not just a little further along in the journey with Jesus but almost a guru. Most of the people I discipled never discipled another person because they felt they couldn't provide discipleship at that high spiritual level, one where it seemed I had all the answers to their spiritual and social needs.

Two, one-on-one discipleship often became more a counseling session than an equipping environment. Counseling a person through a difficulty requires a lot more time, energy, and expertise than equipping them in a discipleship pathway. I have to admit, most of the people I discipled grew a relational dependence on me rather than growing in discipling relationships with others.

Last, one-on-one discipleship did not produce much communal or missional growth in the person. Because group and peer learning wasn't happening nor learning within the context of being sent out together, most of these disciples were limited to a private journey without a place and people to live it out with.

Addressing our underlying assumptions in discipleship requires much unmasking. It requires us as leaders to embrace the hard work of discovering underlying assumptions, structures, and behaviors. It requires us to face the fact that, in the realm of discipleship, we have probably all been dead wrong at one point or another. It's indispensable that we approach peeling back our underlying assumptions with humility in order to reorient our leadership and those we lead and love to make discipleship central.

UNMASKING WITH CHANGE

As we saw in the previous chapter, there are three key components that need to be addressed when we approach change: assumptions, structures, and behaviors. As we move to make discipleship central, we need to assess what our current underlying assumptions, structures, and behaviors are before we identify what kinds of changes are needed and in which direction change needs to happen.

Again, assumptions are any of our current leadership and community's beliefs, habits, traditions, patterns, and paradigms we hold as most valuable to support and live into a given framework. Structures are any policies, procedures, systems, rhythms, resources, and tools that have been built for our assumptions to be implemented. Finally, behavior is the current practice, real-life activity and action, participation, language, common vocabulary, and culture, as well as what the majority of people perceive as the "norm." Assumptions drive structure, which produces behavior.

When we take an honest look at the (Western) church today, what underlying assumptions supported by underlying structures that ultimately default into our current underlying behaviors are keeping discipleship at the periphery? What underlying assumptions about discipleship within our own leadership need to be deconstructed in order for us to move our communities and churches to make discipleship central?

Let's take a closer look at how change theory[1] helps us engage with our own unmasking by touring common behaviors among congregants and leaders (what we do), common structures in place in our churches and leadership (how we do it), and, finally, common assumptions that are upheld in our communities and leadership (why we do it).

Table 8.1. Utilizing change theory to center discipleship

Assumptions	Structures	Behaviors
Question		
Why?	*How?*	*What?*
• Why is discipleship central to our church? Why is it not? • Why is discipleship central to my leadership? Why is it not?	• How are structures set up for discipleship to be central? • How is leadership framed for disciples to be central?	• What tells us that discipleship is central? • What is the tangible evidence in my community? • What is the tangible evidence in my leadership?
Strategy to assess		
Vision	*Calendar, resources, etc.*	*Qualitative and quantitative metrics*
Does our vision clearly communicate that discipleship is central?	Do our calendars, bank accounts, and resources reflect that discipleship is central?	Do we have metrics of character, stories, and numbers that tell us discipleship is central?

What? This question points to behavior, eliciting questions such as, "What tells us that discipleship is or is not at the center of our church?" and "What is the tangible proof in my community and leadership that discipleship is or is not at the center of our church?"

How? This question points to structure and is shaped by questions such as, "How are our structures set up for discipleship to be or not be at the center of our church?" and "How is our leadership framed for discipleship to be or not be at the center of our church?"

Why? This question represents assumptions and asks the questions, "Why is discipleship central to our church, or why is it not?" and "Why is discipleship central to my leadership, or why is it not?"

Without making a concerted effort at this kind of assessment as leaders, we will often misdiagnose a problem or assume the fault lies somewhere else. The truth of the matter is that we often misdiagnose because we don't know how to unmask our own underlying assumptions as leaders. We have good intentions about wanting discipleship to be central, but all too often we have no idea how to be intentional about doing so.

UNMASKING BEHAVIORS

Ask me if discipleship is central to a church, and I'll answer by showing you how its people behave. Behavior is what people do; it's the manner in which they conduct themselves with others and how they respond to the various activities of life.

- In what ways do the people you lead and love behave that tells you they have been discipled or are actively discipling others?
- What is the tangible proof in the life of our church that displays evidence that discipleship is central?
- Do people perceive discipleship—that is, being discipled and discipling others—as a norm in their communal life?
- What are the words they say that let you hear the language of discipleship within the culture of your community?
- In what ways do people engage and participate in discipleship?

In my first church plant, I was hit with the hard reality that discipleship was not at the center of our church. I knew this because the most heralded behavior was Sunday morning attendance, and the second was if enough people were volunteering to serve on those Sunday mornings. Participation equaled attendance, and taking initiative (leadership) meant volunteering. I also knew because regardless of folks coming in large numbers (our church grew to weekly attendance numbers of 450 in just a short time), people were still wrestling with some of the same issues and concerns from the first year. Besides Sunday morning attendance, there was no real marker of a truly discipled life. I couldn't tell if people were just attending church to be entertained, perhaps to hear a good story, or to listen to some inspiring music; or were people attending church because they were actively pursuing a relationship with Jesus and with others? Were folks actually living a more abundant life because of the life-giving love and reign of God in their personhood, or did they return home each week to the same untransformed lives? I honestly didn't know how to answer these questions.

So I began to take a magnifier to our community to see if discipleship was at the center or at the periphery. Instead of asking only if people had been discipled or had ever discipled others (which, as you might suspect, was a resounding no), I began also to ask questions around maturity. In what ways were people behaving in their day-to-day lives? What were they in need of and who were they actually imitating? Their day-to-day lives were filled with anxiety, envy, loneliness, and brokenness; they were in need of vision, healing, and a personal experience with Jesus; they were imitating celebrities and coveting stories of success.

Ultimately, I found that people attended church for one or more of these reasons: morality (I'm a good person because I attend church), self-help (that was a good sermon because I feel better about myself), social requisites (I go to church because that's where my friends are), or spiritual practices (I attend worship service to connect with God). While morality, self-betterment, social clubs, and spiritual practices are good things in and of themselves, participation in these things was not solid evidence that discipleship was central in our church.

Table 8.2. How spectatorship keeps discipleship at periphery

Reasons for church attendance when discipleship is at the periphery	
Experience	*Leadership quality*
Morality	Caring (shepherd—I want to feel loved)
Self-improvement	Charismatic (evangelist—I want to feel popular)
Social club	Clever (teacher—I want to feel smart)
Spiritual practice	

Another note of behavior I paid attention to was what kind of church were people drawn to—specifically, what kind of leadership were people drawn to? This was more than just whether a church subscribed to an attractional model for attendance growth; this was a question about what kinds of leaders attracted people to come under their leadership in the church? If we're really honest with ourselves, people do not attend church because of discipleship; most people "church-hop" or "church-shop" because of the lead pastor.

Christianity Today reports that there are three questions most people ask when shopping for a church: What's most comfortable? What's most agreeable? What's most entertaining? "Unfortunately, the underlying forces driving some church searches are the basic tenets of individualistic consumerism, born out of an assumption that 'church' is primarily a product package of goods and services, designed and marketed to achieve customer satisfaction."[2] Dietrich Bonhoeffer writes that "those who love their dream of a Christian community more than the Christian community itself become destroyers of that Christian community even though their personal intentions may be ever so honest, earnest, and sacrificial."[3] When it comes to leadership and the underlying behavior tied to it, it usually boils down to what people desire (whether our current consumerism or ideal community). People will always seek close proximity to what they need most. And discipleship is not what people think they need most.

In this day and age, people are drawn to pastors who are caring, charismatic, or clever. Folks in need of a sense of care are drawn to shepherd-wired leaders—the proverbial "father (or mother) figure" in their lives. Those who are in need of a sense of trend and bravado will be drawn to a leader who is full of charisma, usually an evangelist-wired leader, because they feel like they're a part of something popular (and entertaining). And those in need of feeling clever and learned gravitate toward the teacher-wired leader because they simply feel smarter. Whether they're providing care and comfort on a weekly basis, imparting a sense of the new style or trend, or dishing out new knowledge week by week, none of these kinds of leaders will naturally put discipleship at the center of their congregations.

UNMASKING STRUCTURES

We then ask the pivotal question of "How?" How are these behaviors supported and perpetuated in our church? It may come as a surprise to consider that we as leaders are setting the structures, whether intentionally or unintentionally, that either encourage discipleship or inhibit it. In my role as a coach and consultant for church planters, re-missioning pastors, and marketplace and community leaders, I have heard my fair share of leaders complain about the complacency of their people (myself included), and I am often convicted of Bonhoeffer's warning in *Life Together*: "A pastor should never complain about his congregation, certainly never to other people, but also not to God. A congregation has not been entrusted to him in order that he should become its accuser before God and men."[4] Many times, more often than not, behaviors of complacency and spectatorship are supported by the underlying structures that perpetuate them. Unmasking structures requires us as leaders to use a keen eye on our systems, rhythms, resources, and tools, our scaffolding of policies and procedures that buffet our people's behaviors.

Discipleship is central or peripheral because of the structures that are in place in our communities. Discipleship cannot be central if there are no structures to support a pathway for discipleship or identifying what discipleship is and who our disciplemakers are. At the end of the day, discipleship is kept at the periphery by structures focused on other things, mainly Sunday morning services. If the primary existence of the church is to esteem the "budgets and butts" metrics of Sunday gatherings,[5] discipleship will always be on the wayside. How we structure our churches, how we set our church rhythms, how we utilize our church resources, and how we equip our community members all pinpoint where discipleship is placed in our church.

Take, for example, the usual process for starting a new church. Just like constructing a new building, scaffolding is required as each new layer of structure is strategically placed. When a new church launches, most church leaders know it's official when they hold the first Sunday public worship service. Even church planters I speak with who have successfully started with their own core discipleship group often believe they have yet to launch—officially launch—their churches because they have not yet held a public worship gathering. Even well-intentioned leaders who are keeping an eye on the importance of discipleship still begin structuring a public worship gathering first, because of a common misperception about the role of a Sunday worship service and its link to discipleship.

Here's how the narrative goes: I am thinking about discipleship because once I launch a Sunday worship service, all sorts of people will come. Once all sorts of people come, they'll hear a sermon, listen to a worship song, and be greeted by an usher in such a way that they'll want to come again. Once they start coming again and again, a sermon, song, or greeting will help them come to a saving knowledge of Jesus and accept him into their heart. Once they accept Jesus into their heart, they're considered a disciple. And that's why a Sunday worship service is important for discipleship.

While I don't entirely disagree with the above narrative and have been a part of my fair share of those types of experiences (I have been to services where the sermon was indeed so powerful that multiple people responded wholeheartedly to commit their lives to Jesus; I have been to services where the musical worship environment was so beautiful and compelling that it caused many to feel a depth of connection with God; I have been in churches where the genuine welcome from church staff and volunteers was the very relational connection people needed to find a sense of belonging), the emphasis I'd like to clarify is where discipleship is placed.

A leader can think about discipleship and keep it at the periphery or at the center. Structuring that places the biggest value on a Sunday worship service isn't devaluing discipleship—it's more likely than not just keeping it in the margins. As much as we would love to believe that discipleship happens in a large auditorium setting with hundreds of people in the seats having just been primed by inspirational music, we aren't really discipling them. We're often simply entertaining them and passing on information. Inspiring is not discipling. Teaching is not discipling. Even exhortation is not discipling. As a teaching pastor in my first church and giving a sermon to nearly five hundred people at a Sunday worship service weekly, I still knew I wasn't making a dent in discipleship. At the end of the day, we know that discipleship is at the periphery of our churches when our churches are structured, calendared, and resourced to support a teaching pastor and a worship pastor to come on stage week after week to deliver their goods to a group of spectators.

I know when discipleship is moving from the periphery to the center by looking at a church's structure, specifically its calendar (what is the regular rhythm of the life of the church), resources (what parts of the life of the church are being funded and why), and leadership (who is being invested in and what are they being equipped to do).

Table 8.3. Centering discipleship requires assessing church structures

Discipleship becoming central	
Church calendar	What is the regular rhythm of the life of the church? Where is discipleship happening in this regular rhythm?
Church resources	What parts of the life of the church are being funded and why? How is discipleship being funded and why?
Church leadership	Who is being invested in and what are they being equipped to do? Are they being equipped to disciple others?

Calendar. When discipleship is moving from the periphery to the center, the calendar of the church begins to change. One church in the Midwest started to restructure itself to make discipleship central by incrementally changing its Sunday worship service rhythm. They slowly changed both the frequency and the content of the services. First they began holding sermon-based gatherings every other week and on the alternating weeks emphasizing prayer and musical worship. Then they dropped one of the sermon-based gatherings and replaced it with a neighborhood backyard barbecue. Then one of the prayer and musical worship gatherings became a neighborhood prayer walk. It took them about a year to do this, but the calendar of this church transformed to once-a-month learning together, once-a-month neighboring together, once-a-month worshiping together, and once-a-month praying for the city together. They were priming their people to become disciples.

Resources. In the same way, when discipleship is moving from the periphery to the center of the church, resources start to reflect the change. Note that I am aware that resources are the most difficult structure to change in most of our established and re-missioning church contexts, because resources are most closely tied to the "ABCs" of church (attendance, buildings, and cash). We operate in a system where we need attendance to be high because only a percentage of those spectators provide a revenue stream that keeps the lights and heat on in our church buildings (let alone providing salaries for our pastoral staff). But when discipleship becomes central, how we use our resources actually does begin to change.

A church in Florida recently acquired a new building and everyone thought the leadership would renovate the space for a grand new sanctuary. Instead these folks started thinking about utilizing the building differently. Instead of putting the focus on the weekly Sunday worship service, they did their main renovation in a multi-use common space where people in their neighborhood regularly came to meet together. Every week the church gathers here, not in the sanctuary, to break off into smaller pods of people based on what their specific needs are that day—some share stories together, others pray for healing together, and still others play games together. Because they changed the resourcing of a physical space, they were priming their people to become disciples.

Leadership. And finally, when discipleship is moving from the periphery to the center of our churches, leadership begins to change. I know that structuring and restructuring for discipleship is happening by looking at: one, who is considered a leader; two, why they are considered to be a leader; and three, how they are being equipped to be a leader. More often than not, leadership in the church is categorized by those who are on staff and those who are not—you're either paid or a volunteer within the church.

Let's look at volunteer leaders, for example. In most churches, you become a volunteer leader (or have paid staff leaders orient themselves according to managing volunteers) based on the different departments of a church. Take a look at any church pamphlet that announces a need for serving in the church. Volunteers can serve in kids' ministry, become an usher or a greeter, or help with setup and breakdown if the church meets in a local elementary school or movie theater. You can even volunteer to be a small group leader. None of these roles are out of the norm; it truly does take a village and a community to keep a Sunday worship service and weekly small group gatherings going.

Structures like this inform a community that those who are able to fill volunteer needs are considered leaders because they have the availability and time to do so and they go through a simple training to fit that role. If you want to be a greeter, please show up at this time and remember to smile. If you want to be a kids' ministry leader, here's the curriculum we use; prep some crafts for them to do and we'll make sure you get a background check. If you want to be a small group leader, make sure you have a home where you can host a group, and pick a topic you want to focus on.

Table 8.4. Discipleship focus: Peripheral versus central

	Discipleship as peripheral	Discipleship as central
Primary focus	We start with public worship and public proclamation.	We start with a discipleship core and a missional community.
Secondary expectation	We expect discipleship to happen from knowing God's Word and worshiping God together.	We expect discipleship to happen through formation within community tethered to local mission.
Tertiary expectation	We have disciples who help grow the church by inviting others to public worship and community outreach events.	We multiply disciples who are vulnerable with one another and proclaim the kingdom of God to the culture around them.

One of the oldest churches in Virginia started to rethink its strategy on leadership and to make some changes to its structure. First, they started turning their small groups into discipleship cores by creating a staff position titled "pastor of discipleship strategies," which meant this paid position was dedicated to developing and implementing discipleship centrally in the life of the church. They also brought in a pastoral resident with a passion for social justice and neighborhoods to help smaller groups of people within the church experiment with practices aimed at assessing the needs of the neighborhoods around the church. One leader was paid to mobilize the entire congregation to begin to think deeply about discipleship, and the other was paid to do beta tests on how the community could become disciples on mission together for the sake of the neighborhood.

Another change this church made was to identify not just the folks serving within the church to support Sunday worship services but those who were serving the neighborhood and community outside the church in intentional Jesus-like ways. Once this small group of individuals was identified, the senior pastor himself carved out time to disciple them in order that they could intentionally disciple others—not to serve the church but to serve their neighbors. Because they changed their leadership structure, they were priming their people to be disciples.

UNMASKING ASSUMPTIONS

Observing behaviors and assessing the structures that support those be-haviors lead us to the point of unmasking our underlying assumptions around discipleship in our communities. Where are we on the continuum of moving discipleship from periphery to center? Where is our church on this continuum? Where is our leadership on this continuum? Most of us have congregations of spectators at worst and volunteers at best, supported by structures and rhythms that use Sunday services as the main way of engaging in the life and ways of Jesus. And we come to the question of why. What is the *why* in your church? What is at the center point of your church that orients the structures and rhythms of your church and ultimately pro-duces evidence of discipleship?

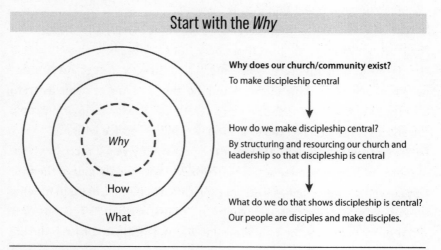

Figure 8.1. Centering discipleship as the *why*

The *why* question helps us uproot our underlying assumptions. These assumptions might be underlying beliefs and values, habits and traditions we've become accustomed to or paradigms and perceptions we hold firmly to. Perhaps our assumptions around discipleship are that people will be discipled by coming to faith in Jesus in large worship services, that people will be discipled by learning from sermons, that people will be discipled by having meaningful worship experiences, that people will be discipled by meeting together regularly at Sunday services, that people will be discipled if they invite their friends and neighbors to our worship services.

If behavior and structures all point to an underlying assumption that the Sunday worship service is the main value in the life of our church, then the question we ask is *why*? Why is the Sunday worship service the centered part of our church?

The *why* question is a leadership question because it has to do with vision. Most churches have some version of the same vision for their communities: our church or community exists to love God and love others. While there's nothing wrong with this statement, especially since Jesus himself deemed it the most important law when he clarified the *Shema* (Mt 22:36-40), in today's day and age, we as leaders need to be more explicit about what this vision means.

For most of our communities, how our people behave and the kinds of structures in place to support those behaviors all display to the world that "loving God and loving people" means running a successful Sunday worship service, week in and week out. Loving God means come listen to a sermon and a song with the word "God" in them, and loving people means invite others to come to a Sunday worship service with me.

It's not a surprise, then, that over the past twenty years, there has been a sharp decline in Sunday service attendance, with nearly half of the individuals in the United States who once identified as being Christian moving to either "non-practicing Christian" or "non-Christian."[6] This has only been exacerbated by the pandemic—it was not instigated by it—during which time it has been estimated that one-third of service-attending Christians stopped attending church altogether.[7]

The current *why* of the church is not working.

If the plan for discipleship is irrevocably tethered to a Sunday worship service gathering, then the plan for discipleship is not working. If the old adage says, "Insanity is doing the same thing over and over and expecting different results," then we as leaders are on the precipice of insanity.

COMPETING POWERS

Before moving on to how we progress out from these assumptions, I want to take this point a little further for leaders. I don't actually think we as leaders are going crazy in the midst of the decline of the church. But I do think part of unmasking our underlying assumptions around discipleship involves uprooting our hidden desires as leaders. If the centrality of discipleship is not a part of the vision for the life of our church, and therefore not a part of our desire as leaders, then we must consider what is competing for that desire.

This topic alone warrants an entire book, but I will offer here that the underlying desires fueling our assumptions (and thereby setting up certain structures that produce certain behaviors) are closely tied to how we view our role as leaders. Am I in this position because I want to be liked? Because I know I can accomplish something significant? Because I want to gain a sense of prestige? Do any of these questions resonate?

- "I can't give up Sunday services because my congregation expects me to give inspiring weekly sermons and I don't want to disappoint them."
- "I can't change up the Sunday service rhythm because my denomination expects me to hit all of my metrics for a successful church."
- "I can't just stop doing Sunday services because I don't have any other qualified leaders."

Whether it's fame or popularity, a sense of accomplishment or productivity, or an ability for command or power, at least one of these areas is likely involved in our underlying desires seeping into the vision for our communities. We have seen, sadly, how desires such as these have devastated many churches and communities, with prominent church leaders enacting unchecked power, abuse of oppressive power, and manipulative relational power.

Table 8.5. Competing powers in leadership

Competing Powers	Relational	Success-based	Authoritative
Competing Desires	I want to be liked	I want to accomplish	I want to be in control
Competing Needs	Popularity	Productivity	Power

I grew up in a Korean American church where there were all too often abuses of cultural patriarchal power and where the desire for fame, accomplishment, and command drove what the community was allowed to do and expected not to do. When I was a youth, our once extremely tight-knit youth group was split in half because our parents became too enmeshed with power dynamics within the church. I remember our youth pastor, with tears in his eyes, gathering all of the youth leaders together and all of us students, sitting down with us in a big circle, to let us know that the senior pastor, elders, and congregation had decided to split up the church.

This was the community I had come to faith in, not because of Sunday worship services but because my youth pastor had made discipleship central to how the youth group operated. While power dynamics ran wild among the adults who had the most social influence, accomplishments, or control, this small band of Korean American teenagers were being equipped to become the next generation of disciplemakers. I do not doubt the grace and wisdom of how God truly does work for the good of all who love him (Rom 8:28), but I know that divisiveness over power should not have been, and it thwarted the efforts of a group of people who loved God and loved one another and were making discipleship central.

UNMASKING LEADS TO TRANSFORMING

As we continue the work of unmasking our underlying assumptions around discipleship, we also make room for transforming our assumptions. As I began to unmask my underlying assumption that one-on-one discipleship was the best way to disciple others, I started to try out group discipleship. It was messy and difficult because I had never done so before. I was uncertain if I could handle all the personalities, questions, and concerns at the same time. I was nervous that one person might be bored or confused while another person gobbled up all of the focus. I started with groups of two to three, then gradually settled into a group of ten to twelve. What I learned from experimenting with group discipleship was threefold. One, it called people to a higher level of commitment, because their responsibility wasn't just to me; it was to the whole discipleship core. Two, the equipping had more depth because the group fed off one another's learning; it provided various and better ways of communicating and understanding the discipleship pathway. And three, the group naturally processed together outside of our regular meeting times, often practicing and discussing discipleship pathway essentials in the real world together.

Since discipling people in discipleship cores, I have not discipled people one-on-one.

9

TRANSFORMING OUR DISCIPLESHIP ASSUMPTIONS

*But Jesus died for our sins not so that we could sort
out abstract ideas, but so that we, having been put
right, could become part of God's plan to put his whole
world right. That is how the revolution works.*

N. T. WRIGHT

*Make every effort to enter through the narrow door, because
many, I tell you, will try to enter and will not be able to.*

LUKE 13:24

MY MIDDLE CHILD WAS ABOUT TEN YEARS OLD when she went
on what she considered a shopping spree. We were in an open-air mall in
downtown Honolulu and her grandparents were visiting from out of state.
As a special gift, Nana told Emma she could pick out whatever she wanted
from the Disney store—in one single flash, this little girl's heart's desire
was being fulfilled, as we had never purchased anything from the Disney
store before!

Now, if you're a person like me who had never even gone into such a store
prior to this momentous occasion, let me give you the setup: you walk in
and are immediately greeted by "cast members" with sparkly mouse ears
atop their heads who usher you into the magical realm and direct you to

merchandise of all varieties with all your favorite characters on them. What would she get? What would she choose? There was the elaborate princess dress-up gown, the deluxe complete set of *Frozen* characters, a backpack that looked like Minnie Mouse, a necklace with a crown pendant, branded pajamas, and endless supplies of character Tsum Tsums! What would Emma decide on?

This was when we realized Emma had a hard time making decisions, especially when she didn't really know what she wanted. She went through the entire store, looking and looking, searching and searching, willing herself to find the most perfect item. In the end she became so overwhelmed with the multitude of options that she came out with a sticker and a cheap plastic water bottle. We were shocked. This little girl, with all the premium Disney options at her disposal, hadn't chosen any of them. As we continued to walk through the mall, I asked her, "Emma, out of all the things in the store, why do you think you chose that water bottle?"

"I just didn't know what I wanted," she replied quietly, wiping the moisture from her small perspiring hands.

That's the thing, isn't it? Even with all the options at our disposal, if we don't know what we want, we won't be able to decide well. If we don't really want discipleship to be at the center of our churches and communities, then we won't know what to do with discipleship. The thing about discipleship is, if it's not at the center, it doesn't work.

After many years of doing church with a focus on the weekly Sunday worship service, I knew I wanted discipleship at the center in my current church plant. And I knew we were about to suffer a lot of losses with that decision—we would stay small for a while, we would forgo corporate worship until we multiplied discipleship cores (which takes years), and we would do life in a way most Western Christians choose not to.

Centering discipleship meant the lines between private and public life would be blurred for those in the discipleship core. It was uncomfortable most of the time. We got on each other's nerves without the respite of a "new person" to help lighten that tension. Centering discipleship meant we weren't going to listen to a sermon together regularly or sing worship songs together. It felt hard to constantly "host" others and not have a place to simply show up. The few times we sang a worship song or hymn together that first year, I wept because of how much I missed it. Centering discipleship didn't just help us learn something new about God, but it deeply examined how our imitation of Jesus was going. We were often met with our brokenness, our lack of love for others, and our intent to build our own kingdoms.

It was unsettling to be confronted regularly by Jesus' call to travel the narrow road: "Enter through the narrow gate. For wide is the gate and broad is the road that leads to destruction, and many enter through it. But small is the gate and narrow the road that leads to life, and only a few find it" (Mt 7:13-14).

CENTERING DISCIPLESHIP

Centering discipleship means we as leaders need to transform our assumptions around discipleship to make it central to the life of our churches and communities. We live in a postmodern, post-Christian world where the culture does not believe that God's Word is true, is suspicious of the rhetoric of tradition and history, and has access to so much uncurated knowledge that anything you want to believe can be backed up by reason and expertise. It most often comes down to what people experience personally. If the mindset is that everyone is entitled to their own opinion and belief, then how do we engage the world around us to create spaces of personal experience where they encounter the depth and width of the love of Jesus?

What happens to a group of people who experience something personally together?

Centering discipleship begins with structuring or restructuring the life of our churches for movement, keeping discipleship at the center. We need to have clarity that this is what we actually want. Discipleship is centered around formation and mission within the context of a community; these are anchoring points for both vulnerability and proclamation to follow. Disciples who are intentionally equipped in the way of Jesus for the sake of the world (neighborhoods and networks of culture around them) cannot help but be compelled by the imitation of Jesus to both be deeply vulnerable with God and others and also to publicly proclaim the beauty, truth, and justice of the gospel of the kingdom of Jesus. Vulnerability and proclamation coincide with being deeply equipped as disciples who live into mission together.

If we as leaders are not compelled by the love of Jesus to live in a new way, then why would anyone else, particularly in our culture today, follow suit? If we're not compelled by the love of Jesus to engage with a changing culture in reimagined ways, then why would our people do otherwise? This kind of leadership takes both boldness and change. And change begins with desiring to reorient our faith assumptions to move discipleship from the periphery to the center.

When discipleship is at the periphery, then our leadership assumptions are that a church worship service meets a person's needs for intimacy with God, personal wholeness, deep connection with others, and participation in the renewal of the community they live in. When discipleship is at the center, then our leadership assumes that discipleship will address a person's needs for intimacy with God. Discipleship will address their wholeness. Discipleship will help them make deep connections with others. And discipleship will form them to participate in God's renewing work in the community they live in.

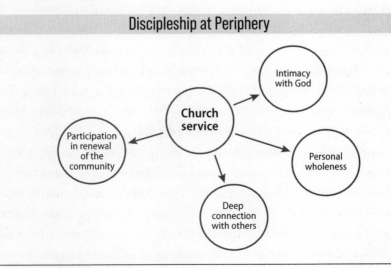

Figure 9.1. Church service at the center

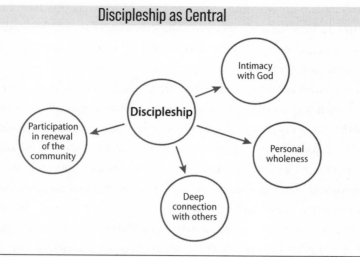

Figure 9.2. Discipleship at the center

DISCIPLESHIP CENTRAL TO ASSUMPTIONS

In previous chapters we examined our underlying assumptions using change theory, and we discovered that assumptions drive structures, which in turn drive behavior. If you want to know what a leader or church's underlying assumptions of value are, just look at the behavior of their members. As we've seen, in most church environments, the most important aspect of being a disciple of Jesus is contributing to the Sunday service, which platforms a main teaching pastor who provides inspiration for Sunday spectators. But what happens when discipleship becomes central to our assumptions? What happens to a leader who makes discipleship their core perspective and value? What happens to an entire church or community that makes discipleship their *why*?

The truth of the matter is that in order to gain clarity that discipleship is really what we want for the people God has given us to lead and love, we have to believe that discipleship is what our people need the most. Being discipled to actively imitate Jesus is the main way people grow in their intimacy with God, find wholeness in themselves, connect deeply with one another, and participate in the renewal work of the cities, neighborhoods, and communities they live, work, and play in.

Discipleship becoming central to our underlying assumptions means we have a new vision that aligns with Jesus' own radical vision of love and life, and we're better able to examine what discipleship can look like in our church communities. What marks of discipleship maturity can we envision in our people? What kinds of lives will our people lead in self-giving love? What kinds of neighborhoods and cultural networks will experience restoration as people begin to actively imitate Jesus?

As we wrestled in my initial church plant with our own awareness of discipleship being at the periphery, I had these questions: Who were the mature disciples in our midst? What made them mature? What about these people showed us they were imitating Jesus? We originally considered that it was due to their faithful attendance to Sunday services, commitment to their small group Bible study, their prayer life, or their ability to know the Bible well, but we began to realize that this wasn't quite it.

Rather, these were people who reflected the character of Jesus: his comfort, compassion, and care. They were full of humility and hospitality and understood the art of long-suffering. They not only read Scripture on a regular basis but rooted their own identity and praxis in God's story. They could easily recall a thought or impression about God in their normal conversations that wasn't overspiritualized but instead came from a deep sense of intimacy with God. They considered God a friend and partner. When confronted by the challenges and detours of life, they were the ones who navigated the complexities well—and well did not always mean being successful or coming out on top but approaching their circumstances patiently, peacefully, and with an assured groundedness. They were also the ones who not only looked like Jesus but acted like him; they imitated the ways of Jesus not just in their own personal lives but constantly in their interactions with others.

While all of these attributes weren't always evident in one singular person, we began to see that maturity in a life that imitates Jesus offered clearer marks than we'd originally thought. Mature disciples of Jesus were those who displayed depth of character in the theology, wisdom, and missional way of Jesus. They behaved, thought, made decisions, and lived their lives in imitation of Christ. Their identity and praxis were deeply rooted in who Jesus is and how Jesus engages with the culture around him. They were simply the ones who gave up their own lives, carried their cross, and followed Jesus wherever he went, always in exchange for something better.

As I began to observe these marks of maturity, I started to identify what new learning we needed in order for discipleship to be central in a way that would produce this kind of maturity in Jesus. We began the deep and necessary work of delineating the core essentials of being a disciple and what was needed to equip our people to become mature disciples in character, theology, wisdom, and missional living.

I remember being in a small group leader's condo in the midst of a familiar scene: me with a flipchart and Sharpie in hand. The question posed to this gathering of our church's small group leaders was this: how do you know you are a disciple of Jesus? They answered similarly to how most leaders, planters, and re-missioning pastors answer this today: I pray, I worship, and I read God's Word.

When I was living in Philadelphia and helping lead a small community church in West Philly, our neighborhood had a mosque at the other end of the block. So we hosted a dinner to mutually learn about Islam and Christianity. In fact, I was attending a Jumaa service weekly to better understand my neighbors and neighborhood at that time. If you were to ask a Muslim the same question, how do you know you are a disciple of Mohammed, they would answer without hesitation: the five pillars of Islam: *shahada* (profession of faith), *salat* (prayer), *zakat* (alms), *sawm* (fasting), and *hajj* (pilgrimage). When the same question was posed to the Christians in that dinner, the night ended with a 101 different answers.

Most Christians don't have clarity about what it means to be a disciple of Jesus. At best we name rote practices that our own people struggle to abide by or find meaning in these days.

Back in that condo living room, I flipped the chart, and there were four blank boxes drawn on the sheet of paper with some themes on them: gospel, personal connection to Jesus, heart for the one, and family of God. The next question went a little further: how do you know you know the gospel, have a personal connection to Jesus, have a heart for others, and are a part of God's family? There was less conversation around praying, attending worship services, and reading the Bible, but the room became a chatter in trying to articulate what the gospel is (Is it a chronological synopsis from Genesis to Revelation? Or just the accounts of Jesus' ministry?), what it means to have a personal connection to Jesus (Is it just prayer? Doing a private contemporary Christian music session in my room? Journaling in the morning?), what it looks like to be evangelistic (Do I have to take a course in apologetics? Start holding a street corner sign with "Repent!" painted on it?), and what in the world God's family looks like (Is this about church attendance? Or small groups?). It wasn't a complete list of essentials, but I knew we were getting closer.

As leaders, once we have an awareness of our skewed underlying assumptions and a genuine desire to make discipleship central, we move from awareness to vision, which leads to new learning (and relearning) and then applying that new learning to a new way of living. In order for a new way of living to occur in our churches and communities, we need to build structures that support and shape discipleship to be at the center rather than the periphery.

DISCIPLESHIP CENTRAL TO STRUCTURES

Most churches are structured around a public Sunday worship service with small groups and community events a distant second and third. In this section we'll look at structuring and restructuring from two vantage points: one as a church plant with the opportunity to start from scratch and second as an established church with the opportunity to make some shifts. In the following chapter, we'll dive further into concepts of structuring to center discipleship in our churches and communities.

Table 9.1. Centering discipleship in church plants and established churches

	Church plant (startup church)	Established church (re-missioning church)
People	Identify and invite those who want to do church a different and smaller way and those who are committed to a similar neighborhood or network	Start with those you have in your church: small group leaders, social influencers, model disciples, those who already have missional intent
Invitation	Share a vision for starting a discipleship core together in your neighborhood or network	Share a vision for starting a discipleship core together as an experiment for increasing discipleship; share a vision for small groups to become missional communities
How to start	Discipleship core using a discipleship pathway	Discipleship core using a discipleship pathway
Don't!	Don't start with Sunday morning service	Don't stop Sunday morning service
Leader's focus	Discipleship pathway	Discipleship pathway
Rhythm	Twice a month for twelve to eighteen months	Twice a month for twelve to eighteen months

Once the leader has a deeper conviction and vision for discipleship to become central to their own leadership and congregation, then structuring can take place. From the vantage point of a church planter, my biggest suggestion is this: *Do not start with a Sunday morning service.* Not even a Sunday evening gathering. And don't think twice about a Saturday night worship service either. Begin with a core group of disciples who already have a commitment to Jesus, are willing and able to make a commitment to a core group of people, and long to be committed to the city, neighborhood, and culture around them. You only need about twelve people to start with who will journey together in a closed group akin to a learning cohort for the next twelve to eighteen months. In that period you will do two things: one, become equipped together through a discipleship pathway, and two, identify a space or place of mission in your neighborhood or network of culture.

The first is for intentionally structured formation and the second is for intentionally structured praxis. Formation and mission, identity and praxis go hand in hand. Soong-Chan Rah, professor of evangelism at Fuller Theological Seminary, notes that time and time again, "where primary and secondary cultures intersect is where the church grows the most."[1] In other words, the Holy Spirit works where a sense of belonging and a sense of purpose overlap—where people find their identity and where they live out their praxis. This sense of mission highlights the presence of God's people going together in community for the sake of the postmodern culture around them, entering into environments where belonging and purpose are both acutely addressed.

If you find yourself in need of a discipleship pathway to equip your core group of twelve disciples, then spend the next three to six months developing one that will move disciples out of their role as church spectators and into a role of active imitators of Jesus. In the meantime, meet with your core of disciples in a set rhythm (once a week to twice a month) and spend that time listening to one another's faith stories and praying for one another. Don't do a Bible study or go through a book—not because these are ineffective but because you are trying to help people reimagine structure in order to make discipleship central. If you start off with a Bible study, it will quickly turn into the same old church small group. If you start off with a book together, it will quickly turn into a Christian book club. The intent of structuring this core group of disciples to meet together in a regularly set rhythm is for equipping them to be formed more and more into the image of the Son (Rom 8:29).

Second, if you haven't identified a space or place of mission yet, spend the next three to six months doing three things:

1. Have each person identify their own personal spaces and places of mission (because one of these may very well become the entire group's core place of mission).

2. Have the entire core group of disciples begin to regularly pray through the city and neighborhood they live in.

3. Have the whole group experience the community and culture together (be guests in the neighborhood).

Figures 9.4 and 9.5 show what my community's calendar looked like the first year.

June 2021

Sunday	Monday	Tuesday	Wednesday	Thursday	Friday	Saturday
		1	2	3	4	5
6	7	8	9	10	11	12
13	14	15	16	17	18	19
20	21	22	23	24	25	26
27	28	29	30			

Figure 9.3. Sample calendar

June 2021

Sunday	Monday	Tuesday	Wednesday	Thursday	Friday	Saturday
		1	2	3	4	5
6	7	8	9	10	☀ 11	12
13	14	15	16	17	18	19
20	21	22	23	24	☀ 25	26
27	28	29	30			

Figure 9.4. Discipleship cores: Group of twelve to fifteen disciples meets together twice a month for twelve to eighteen months to be formed through a discipleship pathway

June 2021

Sunday	Monday	Tuesday	Wednesday	Thursday	Friday	Saturday
		1	2	🍽 3	4	5
6	7	8	9	🍽 10	☀ 11	12
13	14	15	16	🍽 17	18	19
20	21	22	23	24	☀ 25	26
27	28	29	30			

Figure 9.5. Locally rooted mission: Once-a-week community dinners where disciples host the neighborhood to share a meal and a story

June 2021

Sunday	Monday	Tuesday	Wednesday	Thursday	Friday	Saturday
		1	2	🍽 3	4	5
6	7	8	9	🍽 10	☀ 11	12
13	14	15	16	🍽 17	18	19
20	21	22	23	24	☀ 25	🗑 26
27	28	29	30			

Figure 9.6. Locally rooted mission: Once-a-week community dinners where disciples host the neighborhood to share a meal and a story; once-a-month community engagement where disciples are guests in the neighborhood to practice good together

Figure 9.7. Personal rhythm and formation of community mission in the in-between: Disciples practice living into the essentials of the discipleship pathway in their personal rhythms

If you are leading in a re-missioning established church setting, then structuring will look different for you. *Don't stop Sunday morning services.* Our calling as leaders is to both lead and love the people God has given us, and the reality is that once we've done the hard work of gaining awareness and uprooting underlying assumptions, we have often left our people behind. Restructuring is a patient process, one of making incremental bite-size changes that patiently and lovingly wait for our people to experience and transition into those changes. The emphasis is not on rushing them into change; it's on inviting them to participate in change. Instead of rushing headlong into full-scale change, consider first flipping the script on your small groups' primary focus.

The religious landscape in North America is changing, and today nearly two-thirds of established churches have fewer than one hundred people in weekly attendance (over half of churches say they are declining 5 percent per year).[2] From those numbers, one-third of members actively participate in a small group setting. So start with those God has already given you. Begin with two things in your small groups: one, equip small group leaders (or other identified leaders) to become disciplemakers, and two, begin to have small groups identify spaces and places of mission (most small groups are based on geographic location, season of life, or some other affinity).

In my first church plant, we started to uproot our underlying assumptions and move discipleship from periphery to center only after we had been hosting Sunday worship services for 450 attendees. Instead of stopping Sunday morning services, we focused on structuring discipleship within our small groups. Restructuring meant we would take the next three years to turn our small groups into missional communities. In those three years we changed into core groups of disciples, committed to one another, and were intentionally equipped in the ways of Jesus. We took three years to plan to tether our discipleship cores to spaces or places of mission in the neighborhoods around us.

We also intentionally made small groups the biggest focal point in our established church context. We did this through annual quarter-long campaigns that took over our Sunday morning gatherings, emphasizing the key elements of discipleship and the importance of being a part of these emerging discipleship cores, as well as highlighting our discipleship core leaders. Sometimes we would end the service twenty minutes early and send the congregation into the lobby area, which was filled with tall café tables and signs representing every small group/discipleship core/ neighborhood so folks could chat with the leaders and sign up to participate. We changed our sermon series so that more content was conveyed in small group settings. This way people knew they were missing something if they weren't a part of a small group/discipleship core. Each of our small-group-turned-discipleship-core-leaders did a rotation on stage so the whole congregation could hear their stories and relate with these and caring church leaders.

Prior to this campaign, we paused all small groups over the summer so we could take small group leaders away to be equipped in a discipleship pathway weekly. In just three years' time, we had equipped eighty-five small group leaders to be transformed into leaders of discipleship cores in their neighborhoods. Eighty-five percent of our 450-member church was participating in small groups/discipleship cores (and some weeks, we had more people attending our weekly small groups than our Sunday gatherings).

DISCIPLESHIP CENTRAL TO BEHAVIORS

When we as leaders take these courageous steps to grow in our own awareness and vision for discipleship and begin the hard work of structuring and restructuring our churches and communities to make discipleship central, what do we find our people becoming? What will we see our own leadership grow and change into?

At my church in Hawaii, we kept a vision of how people would behave and function as a result of being discipled within a community into the likeness of Christ. The questions we asked were: Are we living in the culture of the kingdom of God? Are we devoting ourselves—being steadfast, committed, and unrelenting in becoming equipped in the way of Jesus, partnering with him and others for a purpose, doing life together in a way that intentionally points to Jesus, and seeking God personally and together as a family? Are we living together in the way of Jesus for the sake of renewal in Hawaii? Are we being formed in the imitation of Jesus and is it showing in our inner person and in renewal of the culture around us? Is discipleship making a difference in who we are, the way we love one another, and how we serve the community around us?

Because discipleship became central to our church, people started living out the imitation of Jesus more fully and specifically in their lives. In our community we don't have a weekly Sunday gathering. In fact, as the lead pastor of our church, I can't remember the last time I gave a sermon. In five years' time, we've grown from a group of fifteen disciples to a group of seventy-two discipled people. We've multiplied from serving a community of fifty people to serving on average 450 people. And we're still growing. We have social spaces in a newly developed "live, work, play" neighborhood, in a condominium, in a neighborhood whose residents have been living there for generations, in three low-income senior living facilities, in a local business, and in a sports community. And we're still growing.

The essential questions that help us tether our discipleship to mission are: "Where are we being sent to?" and "Who are we being sent to?"

Real-life locations and neighborhoods matter to Jesus. Jesus went into real-life locations and neighborhoods all the time, bringing with him the good news of the kingdom of God. We spend time asking God where he is sending us. We spend time asking God where his Spirit is already working. For instance, we chose to locate our first social space in the emerging town of Kaka'ako because of the coming influence it will have on the rest of the city of Honolulu. We next chose the lower-middle-class multigenerational city of Kaneohe because it's where the bulk of local Hawaiian and agricultural family stories are kept.

Real-life people, families, neighbors, coworkers, and friends matter to Jesus. Jesus had conversations with real people and constantly welcomed them into the family of God. We spend time asking God who he is sending us to. We spend time asking God where and in whom his Spirit is already working. We were able to multiply a missional community into a local small business because we were committed to praying for the owners, a couple who have been asking God to use their restaurant to grow a sense of community in their neighborhood. Now even their employees are coming to know and love the faithfulness of Jesus. We multiplied another missional community into a low-income senior living facility because we were praying for the resident manager, someone who used to be a self-proclaimed Satan worshiper who became a disciple of Jesus and is sharing the gospel with the rest of her elderly residents.

Where is your community being sent to? And who is your community being sent to?

Not only did the behavior of our people change from spectatorship to active discipleship, our leadership changed. In making discipleship central, the highest level of leadership wasn't a teaching or worship pastor but the leaders of the discipleship cores. Key church volunteers were no longer the ushers, hospitality team, or setup and breakdown crew for Sunday worship services; they were every person who was being discipled and moving into a real-life space of mission and renewal. We no longer felt moved toward a few non-Jesus-followers occasionally coming to a Sunday service but rather every non-Jesus-follower gaining a sense of belonging and purpose within our open missional communities. What was being multiplied? Not butts in seats but communities on mission together. And what was flourishing over time? Not just the church but the neighborhood and network the discipleship cores were tethered to in their life and love.

While my church that first year gave up an easier way of doing church—listening to a sermon, worshiping corporately together, and just showing up—they made every effort to make discipleship central. Going through a discipleship pathway together in a discipleship core prepared them to be people who understood the gospel deeply and connect to Jesus personally. They not only contended with their own brokenness but developed immense grace for the brokenness in others. They became people who participated in the good news of the kingdom of God and not their own.

PART 4

IMPLEMENTING YOUR DISCIPLESHIP PATHWAY

*Living as Jesus' disciple, I am learning from him
how to lead my life in the Kingdom of the Heavens
everywhere I am, in every activity I engage in. . . .
Disciples are those who, seriously intending to become
like Jesus from the inside out, systematically and
progressively rearrange their affairs to that end.*

DALLAS WILLARD

10

THE FOUR SPACES AND DISCIPLESHIP

Market-driven church that appeals to the materialistic desires of the individual consumer has resulted in a comfortable church, but not a biblical church.

SOONG-CHAN RAH

Yet the news about [Jesus] spread all the more, so that crowds of people came to hear him and to be healed of their sicknesses. But Jesus often withdrew to lonely places and prayed.

LUKE 5:15-16

IN MARCH OF 2020, our church in Honolulu was swept up in the same wave of uncertainties that stopped every church and community. The disruption the pandemic placed on the church at that time affected the biggest event of the church calendar: Easter. Our own disappointment and shock were deepened as we had been anticipating an increase in participants from our Easter gathering the year prior as a burgeoning church plant. In 2019 we'd had over seventy individuals attend our swanky Open Spaces community dinner held at a posh craft-beer-tasting establishment, and we were planning to host over a hundred individuals for this year's event.

We were excited because our missional communities had multiplied, and this was going to be our first collective gathering—the closest thing we would get to a public worship service. I'm not going to lie: it pulled at the right heartstrings and the feeling of finally having arrived as a church plant. Our guests were experiencing a sense of belonging and purpose and our owners were being deeply discipled in the ways of Jesus. This was going to be the perfect gathering to announce that we had made it.

The pandemic messed everything up.

But in the midst of disappointment, I saw the value of centering discipleship. The discipleship pathway our church community was going through shaped not only their formation but also their decisions. They were disciples who moved together toward the community in need. While many of my peers and colleagues were scrambling to learn how to turn their Easter services into a virtual show, our missional communities moved quickly into the neighborhood. One set of disciples moved toward their elderly low-income neighbors and began a campaign that has, to date, provided a month's worth of groceries to five hundred seniors throughout the pandemic. Another set of disciples moved toward the fifty houseless families in their immediate neighborhood and created all-inclusive pop-up "shopping" experiences while thrift stores and soup kitchens were closed due to the pandemic. Another set of disciples partnered with another community serving three hundred houseless people when they heard that their food funding was dropped due to the pandemic. Still another set of disciples responded to the need of local farms for workers due to the pandemic shutting down their internship programs.

While my disappointment over that Easter gathering felt like a loss in that we would not meet the needs of those hundred people, I discovered that our disciples were equipped to face the needs of a much larger population in Hawaii. That Easter and in the weeks and months after, we met the needs of over a thousand individuals.

> But those [seeds] that were sown on the good soil are the ones who hear the
> word and accept it and bear fruit, thirtyfold and sixtyfold and a hundredfold.
> (Mk 4:20 ESV)

Having discipleship central to our church produces disciples who not only are equipped in the ways and maturity of Jesus; it produces disciples who face disruption head-on and navigate through it together. Making discipleship central to our church helps to structure and restructure our community to mobilize disciples into the neighborhood (or network) we are being invited to love.

DISCIPLESHIP REQUIRES COMMUNITY

If community is at the center of what it means to be the church, then discipleship takes shape in the context of community. And if discipleship is shaped within the context of community, then becoming well-versed in how community operates is vital in structuring the church for movement. It's prudent to learn, then, from sociology about how human beings interact in certain social contexts and how spaces of belonging shape community.[1] We as leaders need to intentionally, wisely, and compassionately think about the structures in our churches and communities and consider restructuring to multiply disciples. All of us need to ask ourselves, What are we multiplying? Are we truly multiplying disciples of Jesus for movement, or are we craving a crowd, a social gathering, a Bible study, or easy relationships? Is our aim as leaders and disciplers to shape imitators of Jesus for the sake of the world around us, or are we concerned with getting attendance up for a Sunday morning service?

What are we multiplying?

FOUR SPACES OF BELONGING

Let's establish a common vocabulary before exploring the process of multiplication more deeply. The concept of the four spaces of belonging is a framework borrowed from sociology that explores the social realities of intimate, personal, social, and public space.[2] As JR Woodward writes:

> Jesus lived into the four spaces of belonging in his time. He confided with the three—James, Peter and John (intimate space), trained the twelve (personal space), mobilized the seventy (social space) and spoke riddles or parables to the crowds (public space). If we fail to

understand, appreciate and structure our churches according to these social realities, it will be like going upstream without a paddle. Instead, we ought to imitate Jesus and use these four spaces for the sake of movement.[3]

Because of innate human behavior, each of the four spaces of belonging—intimate, personal, social, and public—cultivates an environment that the other spaces can't deliver on their own. Intimate space of three to four people is the best space to cultivate and build vulnerability. Personal space of five to twelve people is the best space to be equipped and learn together. Social space of twenty to fifty people is the best space to experience a sense of belonging and purpose. And public space of seventy-plus people is the best space for visibility and proclamation to happen.[4]

Table 10.1. Four spaces of belonging

Space	Number of people	Cultivates
Intimate	Three to four	Vulnerability + intimacy
Personal	Five to twelve	Learning + equipping
Social	Twenty to fifty	Community + mission
Public	Seventy or more	Visibility + proclamation

As you can see in table 10.1, a discipleship pathway fits right into the personal space. We have been referring to those journeying together in this way as a discipleship core (bounded set). But in order for disciples to have a place to live out their learning, the discipleship core exists within a missional community (centered set), or, in the four spaces of belonging language, social space. It is helpful for a group of five to twelve disciples (personal space) being equipped in the maturity of Christ through a thoughtful and thought-through discipleship pathway to lead a community on mission together of twenty to fifty people (social space) who are actively engaged with the neighborhood and networks around them in their locally rooted context. JR Woodward continues:

> The beauty of the four spaces is that each space—intimate, personal, social and public—is designed to deliver something the other spaces can't deliver

by themselves. If someone goes to public space and expects to get their intimate needs met, they will be sorely disappointed. Public space (70+ persons) isn't designed to be the place where we share the most intimate things about ourselves. Intimate space (3-4 persons) accomplishes this much better. But if one hopes to build momentum and energy, public space delivers this well.

If one hopes to live on mission with a community of people, where non-Christians can experience a sense of belonging, before having to believe or behave differently, social space (20-50 persons) does this better than any other space. And if one desires to equip disciples to develop the character and competencies of Jesus, there is no better space to do this in than personal space (5-12 persons).[5]

This framework doesn't just apply to the church; we can easily see the four spaces of belonging in the culture around us. Most people who have grown up in Hawaii continue to maintain their friendships from high school, and it's in these circle of friendships, often three to four people at most, that people's deepest longings, sufferings, and joys are expressed. Ask any graduate or MBA student today about the most effective way of learning something in depth, and they'll answer with cohort-based learning, in groups of five to twelve people max. Cohort-based learning can increase student success rates due to interaction, accountability, and collaboration.[6] Charity organizations such as food banks gather groups of twenty to fifty volunteers to help sort and package thousands of food items to be delivered to those in need. Anything less and the work would be too much; anything more and not everyone could participate. Sporting events gather groups of seventy-plus to rally around our teams and be inspired by a shared experience. Any smaller crowd and the inspiration would instantly be diminished.

DISCIPLES MULTIPLY DISCIPLES

Each of the four spaces of belonging multiplies a specific value that deeply shapes disciples, utilizing how people operate in space and community. When our focus is on intimate space, the value of vulnerability—of being known and loved by God and by others—grows, and vulnerable disciples multiply vulnerable disciples. When we put our attention on personal space, the value of being equipped grows, and equipped disciples multiply equipped disciples. When we intentionally utilize social space, a community becomes a community on mission together, and missional and communal disciples multiply missional and communal disciples. And finally, when we focus on public space as not just an idolized crowdsourcing venue but a place for proclamation that the kingdom of God is here and now, then kingdom-hearted proclaiming disciples multiply kingdom-hearted proclaiming disciples.

When we consider structuring and restructuring our churches and communities to make discipleship central, we can use the four spaces of belonging to help identify where discipleship is already central and where it's at the periphery. We can also use it to help clarify which space we put most of our leadership efforts into (and why). We can use it to think about what we long to multiply. Is it public space and our longing for more people to attend our worship services? Is it intimate space and our hope for more lasting friendships within the church? Is it social space and our desire for outreach to happen? Is it personal space and our intent for equipped disciples? We can see more clearly which space is apportioned the most time, energy, skill, communication, finances, and leadership resources.

Which space do you find yourself wanting to multiply and why?

Based on what's being multiplied in your church, is discipleship closer to the center or to the periphery?

MULTIPLYING FAITHFULNESS

Having been involved in church leadership and church planting for over a decade now, I share the common desire to start out focusing on public space. Like many of us, I've spent hours per week preparing for a public space that attempted to equip, connect, and inspire Christians and non-Christians to experience the beauty and depth of Jesus in one hour or less. Hours of training volunteers to be ready for greeting and ushering and doing hospitality ministry. Hours of preparing a sermon that will both captivate and challenge a diverse audience. Hours of agonizing over finances to make sure both church staff and building were secure. In whatever hours were left over, trying to assemble an occasional "outreach" event in order to check off some sort of internal box or in hopes that those reached would increase our public space attendance.

But in pausing and thinking deeply about the four spaces of belonging in my current church context, I took a leap of faith to reimagine church. I'm not always sure how the Holy Spirit works, but I do know that where there is faithfulness to the way of Jesus, he will be faithful to produce fruit. It started with a year of prayer—prayer for our local context, prayer for specific people to come be a part of our personal space, prayer for Jesus to transform our own hearts and character, and prayer for increased grace and ability to forgive one another. From prayer a personal space was formed, a group of twelve men and women who were committed to intentionally live together in the way of Jesus for the renewal of our neighborhood and networks, for the sake of our friends, families, coworkers, and neighbors.

We courageously and faithfully started a social space together and started inviting people to join us in experiencing a sense of belonging and purpose. A year of praying together, then a year of being equipped together though a discipleship pathway while we hosted a social space, and then a year of multiplication. From twelve men and women in a personal space providing intentional community for a group of twenty to fifty people in a social space, we reimagined church together and grew to three different social spaces with growing personal spaces and intimate spaces. We have now multiplied into nine discipleship cores (personal space) tethered to a missional community (social space), and we have begun to host a quarterly public worship space.

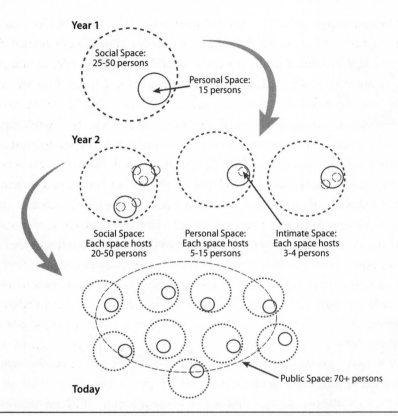

Figure 10.1. Centering discipleship led to first multiplying personal space (discipleship core/ bounded set) tethered to social space (missional community/centered set). Intimate space was formed in a variety of ways: solely within a personal space, a mix of people from both personal and social space, or a group of people formed with those not yet in the community. Lastly, public space started only after we had multiplied personal space tethered to social space five to eight times.

Reimagination of the church has become a reality for us. In my own leadership, I focused on multiplying a personal space tethered to a social space. By doing so, our church has kept discipleship central.

MULTIPLICATION AND STRUCTURE

When beginning to structure or restructure the life of your church for movement, I suggest you start with personal space within the context of social space. If personal space is where formation of disciples happens, then social space is where disciples live into mission together. Dietrich Bonhoeffer writes in his pivotal work *The Cost of Discipleship*, "Christianity without the living Christ is inevitably Christianity without discipleship, and Christianity without discipleship is always Christianity without Christ."[7] If Christianity without discipleship is Christianity without Christ, then discipleship without mission is also discipleship without Christ. If we are to follow Jesus and make followers of Jesus, we must be compelled by his self-giving love and move into mission together. God is a missional God. His very nature of valuing community is tied to mission; the Father sends the Son and together they send the Spirit, who sends his disciples into mission for the sake of the world. If discipleship is about maturity and formation into the likeness of Christ, then there is no formation without mission.

So how does a group of disciples committed to Jesus and to one another in a discipleship core engage with the changing culture around them? How do we lead our communities to live into mission together?

One, our discipleship pathways need to reflect both a heart for and an understanding of the locally rooted context each of our communities live in. Second, a discipleship core (personal space of five to twelve committed disciples) must be actively leading within a space of mission (social space of twenty to fifty people experiencing belonging and purpose together).

Formation does not happen apart from mission. And formation within the context of a community on mission together is an anchoring point for both vulnerability and proclamation to follow. Disciples who are equipped in the way of Jesus for the sake of the world (neighborhoods and networks) around them cannot help but be compelled by the imitation of Jesus to both be loved and known by God and others (intimate space) and publicly proclaim the beauty, truth, and power of the gospel of the kingdom of Jesus (public space). Vulnerability and proclamation are characteristics of deeply equipped disciples who live into mission together.

Personal space starts with five to twelve committed Christians in a closed group who are being formed by a specific discipleship pathway to grow into the maturity of Christ (in character, theology, wisdom, and missional living). Identity in Christ will undoubtedly lead to Christlike praxis for the sake of the world. Social space will be identified and shaped by the mission. Those who are maturing into Christ together can't help but ask these questions:

- Where is God sending us together?
- Who are the people God is sending us to?
- What neighborhood or network is God sending us to?

A sending God sends his people together on mission. Christlike identity leads to Christlike praxis. When a social space begins in this manner, both sustainability and commitment are high.

In my own church, we have structured personal spaces within social spaces in a variety of ways. We have a condominium community where our people host happy hour get-togethers twice a month, with neighbors bringing a chair out to sit and share their lives together. The Christians in that community gather to pray for their neighbors and neighborhood once a month. We have a community in the premier "work, play, live" part of the city, where disciples host weekly community dinners to cultivate a sense of belonging and a monthly social justice work to meet the sense of purpose. The Christians in that community meet together twice monthly to grow together in the way of Jesus. We have a community that loves the elderly and meets at a low-income senior living facility to host dinner and bingo nights weekly. The Christians in that community meet twice a month to anchor their hearts both to Jesus, who compels them to love the "least of these," and to one another. Each personal space is a closed group of Christians who are focused on their formation for mission. Each social space is an open group made up of both non-Christians and Christians who are focused on their place of mission.

A NOTE ON PERSONAL SPACE

I will take a moment to make a distinction between personal space in a discipleship context and the typical small group ministry. The distinction is important not because there is anything inherently wrong with small groups, but because it allows us as leaders to have a fresh perspective on something that seems very familiar to all of us. Historically, small group ministry started with the intent to learn and be discipled together, such as in John Wesley's revolutionary "classes," where groups of ten to twelve people met weekly for spiritual growth in a coeducational experience that not only included women in leadership but those of diverse age, social standing, and spiritual readiness against the backdrop of the "rigid class standard" of eighteenth-century England.[8] In 1935, Dietrich Bonhoeffer started his underground school in Finkenwalde against the backdrop of Nazi Germany to train a small group of young Christian men to defend the truth of God's Word and to learn about the "purpose of our life and work together here, and the special crisis into which the church struggle has led us."[9] When I talk about the difference between discipleship personal space and small group ministries, I'm not referring to what small groups in the church used to be but what they have morphed into today.

Table 10.2. Small groups and personal space are not the same

Areas of difference	Small group	Personal space
Participants	Anyone	Committed disciples
Joining	Just show up	Invite-only
Group	Open or closed	Closed to five to twelve people
Purpose	Participate and grow	Mature and multiply disciples
Frequency	Weekly or every other week	Shared; life together
Focus	Bible study	Discipleship pathway
Learning	Meta-learning	Learning formation
Commitment	Low	High
Engagement	Low to medium	High
Support	Low, medium, or high	High
Stretching	Low	High
Leader	Facilitator	Trained disciple
JR Woodward, "The Fundamentals of Discipleship" (The V3 Movement, curriculum for Year 2 cohort, September 2014), 6.		

Most contemporary small groups are based on a shared learning experience and relationship forming and are open to anyone with interest, whether or not they are a committed follower of Jesus. Facilitated by a small group leader, they are often designed so people can study the Bible or a book together weekly or every other week and participants can recognize a familiar face at Sunday morning service. On average, half of all churches in the United States have fewer than sixty-five people in their weekly worship service, the average church attendance being virtually cut in half over the past twenty years.[10] In addition, it is reported that over 40 percent of those in attendance do not go to a small group; many pastors state the importance of small groups but less than half have a well-defined approach to small group ministry.[11] In this current climate, now exacerbated by the pandemic, clarity regarding small groups is key to centering discipleship. Personal space in discipleship is not the same thing as the current depiction of a small group.

Personal space as a discipleship core is designed to host an environment for purposefully *equipping* disciples to, one, become mature disciples themselves and, two, make mature disciples in others. They are highly committed to the equipping process and to one another through both a discipleship pathway and a shared life together, and they are led by a trained disciple who lives a life worth imitating.

Why is it important? As we have discussed already, discipleship in the church today has become a nebulous term such that most Christians would not know if they had been discipled or how to disciple another person. But if Christ's commission to each and every one (not just some) of his followers is to make more disciples, then it's vital to the life of our churches that we have the ability to equip our community to be just that— disciples who make disciples.

Why is it small? Because the focus of the discipleship pathway is learning formation through a shared life, the personal space requires a group of five to twelve people, no more and no less. It's a social norm that the best group learning environments are these "cohort" sizes of five to twelve individuals—this small number increases commitment because of how much each individual relies on and values each other individual. If you're missing, you will be missed. "The smaller the group is, the more we expect from each other. We expect follow-through on our promises, consistency in our presence, accountability for our actions and vulnerability with our words."[12]

Why is it closed? Because personal space for discipleship formation is shaped in a specific way, newcomers would interrupt and delay the process of equipping, and spiritual seekers may feel uncomfortable and uncertain of the purpose. Both the process and purpose of becoming equipped disciples are of high value in this personal space, and not interrupting them is key to maturation. There's a reason Jesus worked so closely with a closed small group of disciples during his three years of ministry.

What does it look like? The following are some questions that will aid us in moving into praxis:

- Where does the equipping of disciples happen in your church?
- How do you know that equipping of disciples is happening? What are your measurements?
- What kind of discipleship pathway does a disciple in your church follow? If you had to pick the five key essentials in your discipleship pathway, what would they be?
- Who does a disciple in your church learn with? Who does a disciple in your church learn from?

While Sunday service attendance often feels like the ultimate measure of success in the life of our churches, to Jesus, it's the number of equipped disciples who are both imitating him and teaching others to imitate him that matters. Discipleship also always happens not separate from mission but alongside and while mission is happening. The disciples are not equipped and then sent out; they are equipped *as* they are sent out on mission together. Again, personal space happens best within social space— the two go hand in hand. Without the latter, there is no mission, and without the former, there is no formation.

LAYERED STRUCTURE

Once personal space within social space is established, where discipleship includes both formation and mission, my suggestion is to begin to focus on intimate space and public space. Start by asking these questions:

- What are the points within the established rhythm and structure of our church where vulnerability and proclamation can be introduced?

- How do we enfold the regular practice of vulnerability, asking in groups of three to four, "What is God doing in you? What is God doing around you? What is God doing through you?"

- How do we structure a gathering where the spontaneity of the Spirit is honored and the good news of the kingdom of Jesus is proclaimed, news that often comforts the disturbed people and disturbs the comfortable people in our society?

For church planters, it's my recommendation that once personal space—space that enfolds intimate space and lives on mission together within social space—is multiplied to five to eight communities, you're ready to explore public space.

- Where in your neighborhood or network does the truth and beauty of the gospel need to be proclaimed and seventy-plus people can gather together?

- Rather than a musical worship or a sermon, in what ways can you communicate stories about the kingdom of God and invite the Spirit's spontaneous work?

For those leading in established churches, I recommend pausing your current focus on public space—don't stop it, but take some time to re-imagine the structure of the life of your church.

- How can you create personal space within social space to begin to form disciples who are sent on mission together?

- Where do smaller groups of people already feel called in terms of neighborhood, network, cause, or people group?

- How can mission be a connecting point for closed groups of people to gather together to identify the work of the Spirit both in themselves and in these places of mission?

The thing to keep in mind as we utilize the four spaces of belonging to make discipleship central in our church and community is to focus primarily on personal space tethered to social space.

What we primarily focus on, as leaders, is what we intentionally try to multiply.

LAYERED STRUCTURE WHEN
DISCIPLESHIP IS AT THE PERIPHERY

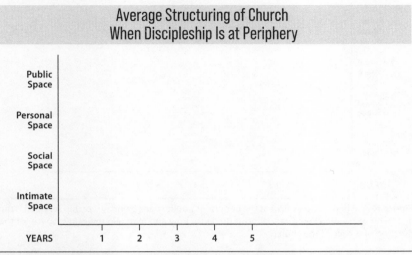

Figure 10.2. Using the four spaces of belonging when discipleship is at periphery

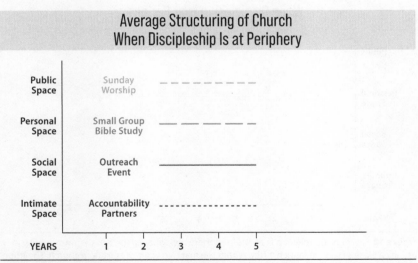

Figure 10.3. When discipleship is at the periphery, public space (seventy persons or more) is Sunday worship services, personal space (five to twelve persons) is small group ministry, social space (twenty to fifty persons) is a church outreach event, and intimate space (three to four persons) is forming accountability partners (and more often in groups of two).[13]

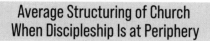

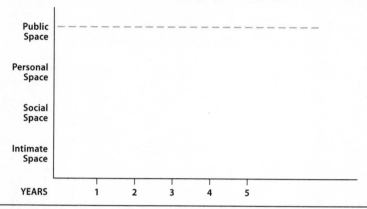

Figure 10.4. When discipleship is at the periphery, public space (Sunday worship services) is the first thing to be launched. Every effort is made to grow and maintain the public space for the duration of the life of the church.

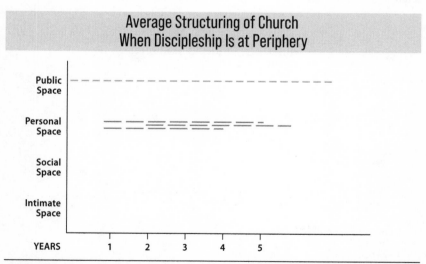

Figure 10.5. When discipleship is at the periphery, personal space (small group ministry) is usually a close second in launch, often within the first two years of starting a church. The hope is that once small groups start, the same small groups will continue throughout the life of the church.

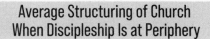

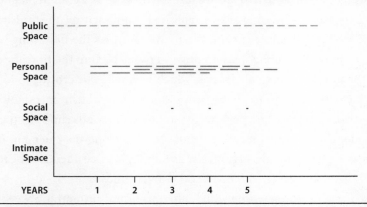

Figure 10.6. When discipleship is at the periphery, social space (outreach events) occurs as a one-off event for the main goal of inviting people to the public space. Most of the time, it happens annually or quarterly at best.

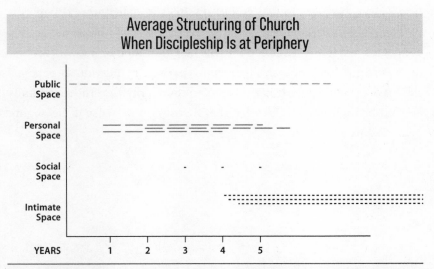

Figure 10.7. When discipleship is at the periphery, intimate space (accountability pairs) starts organically as volunteers and church members begin to become familiar with one another, usually in the fourth or fifth year.

When it comes to structuring our churches, we often utilize the four spaces of belonging in this manner: public space is our Sunday worship service and our main event. Whether we are just starting out as a church plant or receiving the baton of leading in an established church setting, the pressure to uphold the public space is common for all of us. It's the first thing we do. We count on the public space to draw a crowd. Next in the timeline is the personal space, our small groups, which we invite our crowds to join if they have some time for fellowship. Once we establish an ongoing Sunday worship service and perhaps get some small groups running, then we consider doing some outreach events studded along the calendar. Intimate space often happens organically as Sunday service attendees begin to familiarize themselves with one another over time.

While there's nothing wrong with highlighting and sustaining a weekly proclamation, this kind of calendar doesn't necessarily make discipleship central. Discipleship is probably happening, perhaps in one-on-one settings and pieces of discipleship content within the sermons, but intentional clear discipleship that equips disciples to make more disciples is probably not intentionally happening. Second, discipleship is not getting connected to a sense of mission into the neighborhood or network around us. Again, mission is probably happening, perhaps in individuals' personal rhythms, but not regularly in the gathered church rhythm. The community is often being invited to a crowd that focuses on its sense of belonging, being inspired by Jesus.

LAYERED STRUCTURE WHEN
DISCIPLESHIP IS AT THE CENTER

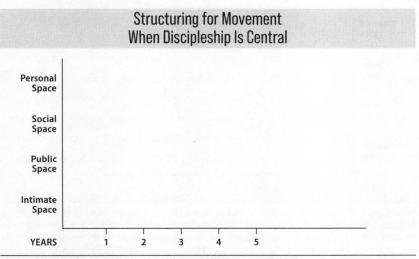

Figure 10.8. Using the four spaces of belonging when discipleship is central

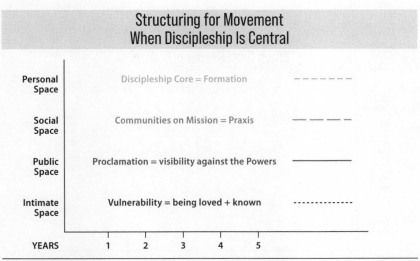

Figure 10.9. When centering discipleship, personal space (five to twelve persons) is a discipleship core, and its focus is on Christlike formation; social space (twenty to fifty persons) is a missional community, and its focus is on Christlike praxis; public space (seventy or more persons) is a gathering that focuses on proclamation and bringing visibility against the powers; and intimate space (three to four persons) is an intentionally formed group that is larger than a pair that focuses on practicing vulnerability and being known and loved by God and others.

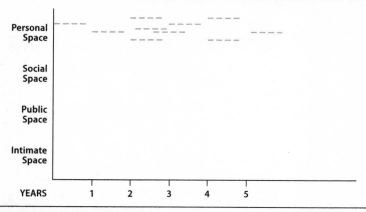

Figure 10.10. When centering discipleship, personal space (discipleship core) is the first thing to focus on. As indicated here, discipleship cores run through a course of twelve to eighteen months and end after the discipleship pathway is complete. The same discipleship core does not go on for years because the aim is not to form relationships but to be formed into the likeness of Jesus within a community. Discipleship cores multiply, start and end, over and over again throughout the life of the church.

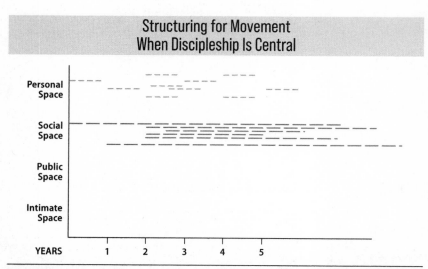

Figure 10.11. When centering discipleship, social space (missional community) starts ideally simultaneously tethered to a personal space (discipleship core). Social space is where the sense of belonging and purpose are met for both a Jesus-following and non-Jesus-following community of people. It's the space that has the most longevity and aim for sustainability.

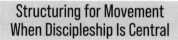

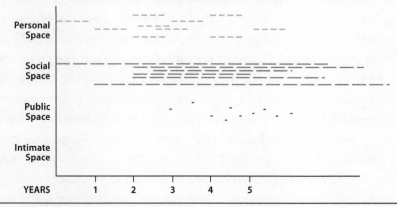

Figure 10.12. When centering discipleship, public space (gathering for proclamation) is what is studded in a timeline. In my church, once we multiplied to five personal spaces tethered to social spaces, we launched a public space with the goal of holding a gathering of seventy or more persons once a quarter only. We did not start a public space until the third year.

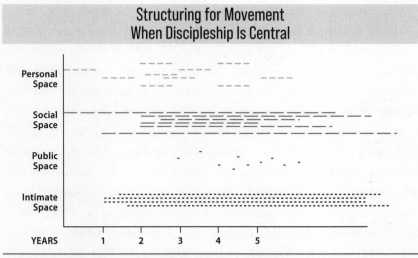

Figure 10.13. When centering discipleship, intimate space (groups of three to four for vulnerability) intentionally starts after first establishing a personal space tethered to a social space. It purposefully makes space for disciples who are being formed and practicing imitation of Jesus together to have a vulnerable and honest space to examine and experience the knowledge and love of God and others.

When we as leaders keep discipleship at the center, we think about structuring the church differently. We often start with (and in established settings, intentionally form an additional) personal space, the discipleship core. In the timeline, we quickly tether it to a social space, the missional community. This kind of structuring emphasizes the importance and centrality of discipleship and connects formation to mission. It also presumes that discipleship does not just happen in individualistic ways; it happens within community. Once those two spaces are established and multiplied (five to eight discipleship cores tethered to a missional community), then hosting a public space makes sense (five personal spaces would have fifty to sixty disciples who are leading 100 to 250 members within social spaces). We would be inviting seventy-plus people into an environment to draw inspiration from and hear stories of how God is actively on the move within all of our communities. Intimate space often forms for disciples in personal space together, sometimes a combination of people in the discipleship core (personal space) and in the missional community (social space), or from other communal environments.

The first time my church in Hawaii hosted a public space, we gathered all of our missional communities together for a backyard worship night (seventy people were in attendance). For three years we did not host a public worship space, because it took three years for our church to multiply into five personal spaces tethered to a social space. It was the first time in three years that we heard a sermon together, took Communion with a large group, and sang in corporate worship with that number of people. We wanted to be intentional with our time together and did not just want to draw a crowd for crowdsourcing's sake; instead, we had each of the missional community leaders lead Communion at their own tables with their own community, and the sermon was a dialogical style of preaching where we had conversation around our missional community tables to identify the powers at work in our unique neighborhoods. We prayed and worshiped together to contend against the powers of idolatry, isolation, and ideology. We asked God to help us unmask the spirit of this world that comes to steal, kill, and destroy. We asked God to help us participate fully in the abundant life he invites us into (Jn 10:10).

The beauty of a personal space or a discipleship core is that it unequivocally meets the need for disciples to be equipped in the ways and maturity of Jesus through a discipleship pathway. Equipping and discipling don't happen best in a public space, no matter how skilled an orator and teacher we are. We can inspire and inform, but we will not provide a setting for formational incarnational practice. Equipping and discipling will not happen effectively in intimate space either; the smaller the space, the better it is for peer accountability, counseling, prayer, and iron-sharpening-iron work. We can experience the knowledge and love of God for one another through reflection and vulnerability, but it is not the place to learn and practice.

In our local context, keeping our discipleship core closed was a difficult decision to make, especially since we wanted to grow in numbers. It can be a lonely road to plant a church. That first year journeying through a discipleship pathway together twice a month we constantly fought the urge to open it up—why wouldn't we when we wanted to share what we were learning and invite others to feel "spiritually fed"? I'll admit, we didn't do this perfectly all the time. I remember a few times when we opened our discipleship core up to a new guest midyear who wanted to "try out" the discipleship pathway. It instantly changed the room. It was like having a level-one Spanish student come join in a graduate-level Spanish course. The entire group changed its course from learning to accommodating.

Similarly, the beauty of a social space or missional community is that it unequivocally provides a sense of belonging and purpose for a new person better than any of the other four spaces. A new person coming into community will often slow down the equipping process found in personal space (five to twelve people) and confront the uncertainty of whether or not they fit in. A new person entering into an intimate space (three to four people) will quickly halt the value, confidentiality, and safety of vulnerability. And a new person showing up in public space (seventy-plus people) will be easily missed and unintentionally dismissed.

But in social space (twenty to fifty people), the new person can naturally find those they can connect with and those they can move into meaningful work with. They can experience a comfortable level of figuring out the community and trying out different ways of fitting in while simultaneously being welcomed personally into meaningful relationships and meaningful purpose. In social space, people are acknowledged and can contribute.

In our local context, we have a regular rhythm where our social space becomes guests from another organization, small business, or cause in the neighborhood. For instance, we'll bring a group of about twenty to fifty people to volunteer together at the local food bank; we have found that this partnership toward meaningful community service has been one of the biggest draws for both Christians and non-Christians, especially in a post-pandemic world where we have lacked purpose and belonging. It's easy for new people and regulars to join this work together, and our main focus is not to get the food packaged but to intentionally make meaningful relationships with our neighbors. Each of our guests' presence matters without disrupting confidentiality (intimate space), progression of learning (personal space), or proclamation (public space). Each person can fully participate in the community and mission at hand (social space).

A discipleship core (personal space) that leads and shapes a social space moves an entire community toward a sense of belonging and a sense of purpose compelled by the love and reign of Jesus. In social space, Christians and non-Christians share life with one another and work together for the renewal of the neighborhoods and networks around them.

Structuring and restructuring takes time, but it is time worth spending if we want to genuinely participate in the movement Jesus calls us to. Exploring, identifying, and practicing discipleship through the four spaces of belonging will not only transform the disciples in your church, but it will actively renew the culture and communities around them and spur on movement to love and follow Jesus. "For Christ's love compels us, because we are convinced that one died for all, and therefore all died. And he died for all, that those who live should no longer live for themselves but for him who died for them and was raised again" (2 Cor 5:14-15).

11

HURDLES TO DISCIPLESHIP

Far too many people, especially within evangelicalism,
think that the individual is all that matters, and that the
corporate dimension is a distraction or diversion.

N. T. WRIGHT

Another disciple said to [Jesus],
"Lord, first let me go and bury my father." But Jesus told him,
"Follow me, and let the dead bury their own dead."

MATTHEW 8:21-22

WHAT COULD BE MORE MOTIVATING THAN an invitation to become part of a community that intentionally moves into mission together for the sake of their immediate neighborhood and network? What could be more compelling than an invitation to join in the work of restoration of identity, purpose, goodness, beauty, justice, and truth for ourselves and those around us? What could be more captivating than an invitation to live a life with intent, being deeply discipled into the likeness of Jesus alongside a group of people who are also being deeply discipled into the image of Christ?

The truth is that it isn't as motivating, compelling, or captivating as we as leaders think. The real work begins when we face hurdles as we move from developing a discipleship pathway to inviting others into it.

Within the next ten years, it is estimated that one-third of Canadian churches will close their doors.[1] A third of current Christians admit that they attend weekly Sunday services infrequently, while 44 percent feel that attendance is not that important. And in the midst of Covid-19, a third of Christians stopped attending church altogether.[2] Over the past half century, the Western religious landscape has been shifting, with every single Christian denomination or other faith group, including Judaism and Islam, declining or flatlining. Only one belief system continues to experience exponential growth: postmodernism.[3]

The days of thinking that a Sunday morning church service will compel a changing culture to adhere to the new life Jesus offers us are numbered. And a global pandemic that has produced political, social, and economic polarization and social injustice makes a focus on "filling the pews" trite at best. We are on the precipice of restructuring and reimagining church. In being shaped and transformed into the image and imitation of Christ, we must both be and make disciples who are compelled by the love of Christ and follow him in a way "that those who live should no longer live for themselves but for him who died for them and was raised again" (2 Cor 5:15). As church pastors, church planters, and community leaders, we must equip the disciples God has given us to love and lead to engage with an ever-growing postmodern culture. We must not hole up in the safety and comfort of our Sunday morning services but go out on mission together for a world in need of the beauty and life-giving rule and reign of God. Discipleship cannot happen apart from mission. And invitation cannot happen apart from vision.

Even if we've devised a five-star discipleship pathway and embedded it into the perfect structure within our church or community, it's not a given that people will want to participate. Every entrepreneur and startup knows that even if they've built an ideal product, if people don't engage with it, the product will become obsolete. If a discipleship pathway isn't being used to make more disciples, it will become obsolete. If a discipleship pathway isn't producing an environment of flourishing for the local community around the group of disciples, it will become obsolete. A discipleship pathway must be connected to disciples.

Our youngest daughter, Kyriella, is a fish. She's the first in the ocean and last out. In the coldest Hawaiian months, she's often the only one in the water. She loves most the people who will join her in the water and comes back out only when her fingers and toes can compete against the wrinkliest of prunes. She stays hours in the pool and, if there's a slide involved, even better. But she wasn't always like this.

When Kyriella was about two years old, we were at a pool with a great big yellow slide that splashed out into a small four-foot-deep opening. She smiled as she watched her older siblings go down the slide, but every time we invited her to come, she shook her head and refused. Nothing could convince her that she would actually enjoy the slide.

"Kyriella, you're going to love it!"

"No!"

"Kyriella, it's so much fun!"

"No!"

Each invitation was met with a progressively louder "no!" until my husband gently took Kyriella in his arms and proceeded up the stairs to get in line for the yellow slide. She was beside herself. Our usually quiet and sweet youngest child turned into a howling banshee, and with each step she ramped up the volume of her cries. At the top of the slide, my husband's face was flushed with shades of "Everyone must think that I'm a terrible father," while Kyriella persisted in her wailing and I waited for her at the bottom of the slide. As he gently nudged her forward, she roared the loudest of her bawls, but just as suddenly, her cries turned into a squeal of laughter and a great big "Yippee!" As I waited for her at the bottom, she was sitting straight up as she gently rolled down with the slide water. She leaped victoriously into the pool and splashed over to me. "Again! Again!"

Needless to say, Kyriella spent the rest of that day sliding down that big yellow slide with her siblings. She overcame a huge hurdle that day at the pool. Overcoming hurdles is commonplace in childhood, but it's also very common in discipleship.

One woman in our church's discipleship core had quite a few hurdles to overcome herself. Callie had recently changed careers, had two young children at home, was dedicated to her sleep and fitness schedule, and barely had time to engage with her husband, let alone friends. Her eyes began to well up with tears as she felt overwhelmed by the commitment to the discipleship core. When she started a mental list of what needed to go, she kept contemplating withdrawing from the discipleship core. She couldn't take out family, work, or health.

Callie wasn't alone in wrestling with this hurdle; many people are confronted by the constraints of everyday life. So how do we address this and other common hurdles to discipleship? How do we gently nudge people forward as we invite them into the process of being discipled into the beautiful way of Jesus so those around them will also thrive?

HURDLES COMMON TO EVERYONE

The first step to forming a personal space tethered to a social space, or a group of committed Jesus-followers on a discipleship journey together, is invitation. And invitation comes with its own challenges. In all of my conversations with leaders and pastors, these three hurdles are the hardest to overcome when forming a discipleship core: a lack of commitment, a culture of complacency, and limitations with children. As we address each of these hurdles, we'll ask the following questions:

- What does this hurdle look like in people's behavior?
- What structures and systems are in place that support this hurdle?
- What needs to change in order for them to overcome this hurdle?

Hurdle of commitment. Commitment in our postmodern Western culture is elusive at best. In a world where priority is reserved for the "next best thing" and spontaneity is more attractive than having our calendars locked in, gaining assurance of people's presence is not a given. There is an epidemic in our culture of unwillingness to commit that affects how people make decisions. And a decision to be discipled is not exempt from this.

What does a lack of commitment look like? It's saying yes to something and then not showing up. It's apologizing at the last minute that something came up. It's not responding to an invitation until the last minute—or at all. Even if I physically attend, I may not be emotionally or mentally present; I may withhold information or refuse to participate.

And even if I do engage, I may be unavailable in the in-between times and won't do the work of processing. At the heart of this behavior pattern is a struggle with selfishness. And selfishness is something people can be gently pulled out of via small steps. We do not confront selfishness with condemnation, aggression, or guilt. We meet it with understanding and a vision for community.

Most noncommitting individuals on the one hand live within a millennial cultural expectation that it's okay to hold out until something better comes their way.[4] On the other hand they have an individualistic mindset that doesn't want others meddling in their personal lives, personal decisions, or personal schedules.[5] Selfishness says, "It's more beneficial to me to not say yes until I'm certain this is the best thing for me. What if something better comes along? I don't want to miss out!" Selfishness also says, "I don't want to get into a situation where I may lose control—control over what I can and cannot do, control over how I make decisions, and control over my time. I don't want to lose control over my own life!"

There are often key structures and systems in place supporting an absence of commitment that's motivated by selfishness. These structures and systems uphold an individualistic consumer mindset wherein we as church leaders build programs and incentives into our invitations to try to convince people that discipleship will be worth their while. We feel driven to entertain instead of equip, and discipleship becomes distorted into a feel-good experience where people can come and go as they please. It is no longer an invitation into a journey with Jesus. We provide programs over process and individualized, privatized, self-help religion-in-a-box instead of communal growth in faith, hope, and love.

The change that needs to occur in order for people to overcome this lack of commitment is a clarity of vision of community and mission—a clear answer for, "Who's doing this life with me and what in the world are we doing together?" To face this hurdle head-on is to paint a clear picture of community. Why? Because community is what will lead them away from selfishness and toward selflessness, toward a transformed life of thinking of others first—both those we walk alongside and those we walk toward.

Hurdle of complacency. A culture of complacency is another common hurdle leaders must overcome when inviting others to be discipled together for the sake of the community around them. Complacency in our Western culture has very little to do with true contentment. While on the surface complacency may seem like a choice for ease over hardship, on further examination we find that it is actually more likely a response to uncertainty: avoidance, abdication, absent-mindedness, anxiety, or some combination of these common reactions to uncertainty.

Avoidance shows up as repression (burying emotions, concerns, fears, and vulnerability), numbness (detaching from others, which blocks the ability to confront, process, and problem-solve), or addiction (distraction through binge-eating, -watching, -drinking, etc.). As Brené Brown says, "We emotionally 'armor up' each morning when we face the day to avoid feeling shame, anxiety, uncertainty, and fear. The particular armor changes from person to person, but it usually revolves around one of three methods: striving for perfection, numbing out, or disrupting joyful moments by 'dress rehearsing tragedy' and imagining all the ways that things could go wrong."[6] Abdication presents itself as compliant inaction—giving up responsibility, concern, or engagement and waiting without contribution until a hardship goes away. It seems that a large percentage of supposed Christians have chosen abdication as their strategy for surviving the spiritually toxic environment of this world. They throw in the towel of concern, compassion, and subversion. Since it's just easier to not care, they surrender. Absent-mindedness is a form of denial—being unaware of the implications of current circumstances on oneself or others or having an inattentive and oblivious disposition. And finally, anxiety shows up as overwhelming paralysis—an inability to shift well to situations and people, mourning over what could have or should have been, having broken expectations, and exhibiting overcompensating behavior.

Even a quick glance at society tells us that complacency is well-supported by structures and systems. A culture riddled with distractions and endless choices will convince anyone that they always have the option for ease and comfort. And the same culture will inhibit a person from uncovering the realization that their complacency really stems from fear and uncertainty.

The change that needs to occur for people to overcome the hurdle of complacency is to address the uncertainty. Complacency is invariably a mask we don to avoid being confronted by uncertainty and change; therefore, its relief comes through certainty and assurance. Those who wrestle with complacency are constantly asking the question, "What will I lose in this decision?" And we see Jesus pinpointedly address this question:

> If any of you wants to be my follower, you must give up your own way, take up your cross, and follow me. If you try to hang on to your life, you will lose it. But if you give up your life for my sake, you will save it. And what do you benefit if you gain the whole world but lose your own soul? Is anything worth more than your soul? (Mt 16:24-26 NLT)

Jesus very plainly shares that discipleship—being truly discipled and formed and reformed into his very likeness—involves loss, discomfort, and a willingness to give up control of our own life. But Jesus also reveals that transformation happens through giving up our own life to do life with him, returning abundance to us thirty-, sixty-, a hundredfold.

Hurdle of children. Our final hurdle to discipleship is that of limitations with children. This is probably one of the most frequent questions I've received as I've walked with leaders and pastors—how do you invite people into a discipleship pathway if they have children? What do you do with the kids even if their parents say yes to being a part of a discipleship core? What curriculum do you use for children and how did you get a children's minister? This hurdle is twofold: adults being "fed" without distraction and children being "fed" at church.

Most church environments handle this hurdle by hosting a separate place for children's instruction. Because most of our church structures are laid out to support the Sunday worship service primarily, we curate a children's Sunday school program in order to, first, remove distraction and, second, teach our children biblical lessons. In 2022, Barna surveyed over two thousand adult church attendees and six hundred Protestant church leaders in the United States; the organization reported that two-thirds of parents select a church based on its children's ministry and two-thirds of leaders strongly agree that "churches cannot grow without an effective children's ministry."[7]

Our current structures assume that children cannot participate in adult discipleship and the church is the main discipler for children. In essence, church structures support isolation and separation; restructuring needs to consider inclusion and participation.

The change that needs to occur in order for people to overcome this hurdle is to grapple with the difference between isolation and inclusion. While most church environments promise an hour of babysitting (with a side of Bible lesson) for parents and guardians, the truth of the matter is that we should be asking who we're discipling. Does the discipleship core consist of families with young children or is it multigenerational? Is the discipleship core made up of mostly young professionals or are there school-age children involved? The rules and rhythm for discipleship in a particular discipleship core depend very much on who said yes, and the beauty of a discipleship pathway is that while the essentials are steadfast, the tools and scaffolding around it are flexible. Holly Catterton Allen and Christine Lawton Ross write:

> Most churches and faith communities segment their ministries by age and generation. . . . Worship services are geared toward different generational preferences. . . . In some congregations, people may never interact with those of other ages. But it was not always so. Throughout biblical tradition and the majority of history, communities of faith included people of all ages together in corporate worship, education, and ministry. The church was not just multigenerational; it was intergenerational, with the whole church together as one family and people of all ages learning from one another in common life.[8]

The first year we started out, we had fifteen adults, a mix of older and younger people all in varying stages of life, and nine children. Because our rhythm together was to do a weekly open community dinner in the heart of Honolulu as our place of mission (social space), our closed discipleship core (personal space) only met every other week (twice a month) for intentional equipping and journeying through our discipleship pathway together in twelve months. This first year, we set up our structure keeping inclusion in mind. All of our open community dinners were purposefully designed so they were always welcoming to children of all ages; in fact, the kids hosted a discussion table for themselves and quickly moved into an indoor foursquare match or soccer with loads of giggles and squeals. They were forming an open, welcoming community for children on their own. The older kids led the discussions and swiftly learned to keep it short; they even learned to include a little girl with a physical disability. Adults in the discipleship core who naturally had a passion for children without fail joined the "kids' table," but it was led by the children. Because we knew that in our budding community there was a clear place for children, we could change up the structure for the discipleship core, and we were led by the purpose of the discipleship core—which was for equipping and learning.

This led us to the question, "How old do you have to be to be able to be equipped and learn as a disciple of Jesus?" We came to the developmental learning age of eight years old. If this was the case, then we also knew that our discipleship pathway had to be simple enough for a second grader to understand and deep enough for the most mature follower of Jesus to still be challenged. And because the discipleship core only met twice a month, we had clear conversations with those with younger children to set up babysitting. The twice monthly personal space truly became an environment for learning, growing, and maturing, and the weekly social space became an environment for communing, serving, and practicing.

Table 11.1. Hurdles to forming a discipleship core

Hurdles to discipleship	Heart behind the hurdle	How to help the heart
Commitment (lack of)	Selfishness (opting for something better or control)	Vision of community and mission
Complacency (competing culture)	Comfort (responding to uncertainty with avoidance, abdication, absent-mindedness, or anxiety)	Vision with certainty and assurance
Children (limitations with)	Distraction (wanting to be "fed" without interruption)	Vision for inclusion

OVERCOMING THE HURDLES

These hurdles of lack of commitment, a culture of complacency, and limitations with children can be met with a tool called "the five Cs of discerning a discipleship core."[9] The five Cs (character, compatibility, competency, capacity, and confidence) give us a way to tell if a person is able and available to commit to a discipleship core and journey through a discipleship pathway. As we've already explored, a discipleship core (personal space) that is tethered to mission (social space) must have a high commitment level from its people in order for deep discipleship within community to actually happen. It takes a devoted, closed group of people (ideally five to twelve people) who desire to grow in their commitment to God, to one another, and to the city (neighborhood or network) God has placed them in. And commitment takes discerning.

Simply put, character pertains to the disciple's imitation of Christ's own character, as displayed through the gifts of the Spirit (Gal 5:22-23). A person of character is faithful, servant-hearted, a lover of people, a peacemaker, humble, hospitable, generous, pure of heart, joyful, patient, and self-controlled. Compatibility marks a person who is able to do life with others in thick community, despite differences in temperaments and preferences, with self-awareness and grace extended toward others for the sake of unity, not conformity. Competency points to a person's adeptness in discipleship, and in our context, it means the ability to be equipped through the discipleship pathway and its holistic competencies and essentials. Capacity has to do with a person's scope in life and whether they can make room for a discipleship pathway in the midst of a given season or stress. Confidence reflects a personal vision, a plumb line of commitment to Jesus, to the discipleship core, and to the flourishing of the community around them.

Table 11.2. Five Cs of discerning a discipleship core

The five Cs of discerning a discipleship core	
Character	Does this person reflect the likeness of Jesus through discipleship?
Compatibility	Is this person able to do life with others in a discipleship community?
Competency	Is this person able to be equipped through a discipleship pathway?

Capacity	Does this person have the scope and space to be on this discipleship journey?
Confidence	Is this person convinced of the vision for discipleship?

As leaders, we can use the five Cs tool to do an astute assessment of individuals, but in general, when it comes to dealing with people's common hurdles, we can boil it down to just one C. The first three (character, compatibility, and competency) all fall into the category of self-disqualification.

"I don't know if I'm the right person for this."

"I don't know if I know enough about God to do this."

"I don't know if I know how to do this."

These responses and hesitations are all in the same category: growth. A discipleship pathway, designed intentionally for disciples of Jesus to mature into the likeness of Jesus' character, theology, wisdom, and missional living, specifically means disciples are not yet great at any of it; they are be equipped and growing in these areas. From weakness to strength. From immaturity to maturity. From limited-us to more-ourselves-us through the imitation of Jesus. Character, compatibility, and competency are all intentionally addressed through the discipleship pathway. Disciples are invited to grow in their character in a way that reminds others of Jesus, compatibility and grace with and for others because of Jesus, and competency and maturity in living in the ways of Jesus.

The last two Cs help us better address the hurdles people face when committing to a discipleship core: capacity and confidence. These are tricky criteria in our postmodern world. Despite our calendars getting packed, we want to own the rights to our time even as workaholic tendencies and time-consuming addictions take over our schedules unplanned. Our culture, which demands performance and pleasure, makes capacity and confidence conversations difficult. I have personally experienced having something highly meaningful planned for my church community and at the last minute receiving a barrage of texts stating that other things had "popped up" unexpectedly, that it had been a "hard day" so they needed to cancel, that I hadn't given them enough advance notice, or that they'd completely forgotten about it. The difficulty with capacity is better addressed through motivation. Motivation is where vision casting comes in, and vision is how confidence is addressed. Commitment has to do with clarity in vision, and vision sets priority.

Table 11.3. Discipleship and vision address hurdles

Five Cs of discerning a discipleship core		What addresses this?
Character	Does this person reflect the likeness of Jesus through discipleship?	Discipleship in the maturity and likeness of Jesus
Compatibility	Is this person able to do life with others in a discipleship community?	Discipleship tethered to a community
Competency	Is this person able to be equipped through a discipleship pathway?	Discipleship through a discipleship pathway
Capacity	Does this person have the scope and space to be on this discipleship journey?	Vision for discipleship
Confidence	Is this person convinced of the vision for discipleship?	Vision for discipleship

In my own experience, capacity, although it appears to be about a person's calendar, has more to do with passion. Passion is more motivating than a calendar, and we fill our schedules based on prioritizing the things we feel we must do (work, obligations, and things that can result in consequences) and then the things we want to do (hobbies, recreation, and the things that result in pleasure).

Early on in one of my ministry contexts, I gathered leaders who would begin to disciple people. We were starting out by discipling others one-on-one. I planned a discipleship equipping session for these leaders so our community would all be on the same page, and it would take no more than two hours. I invited one man who was an influential leader in our community into this core group of disciplers, but he just couldn't make the time to come to the gathering. He was a husband and a father of young children trying to make ends meet. His calendar seemed at capacity, and while he really longed for deeper discipleship to happen, he just wasn't in the season to be able to commit to a two-hour equipping.

But the funniest thing happened. I also planned an impromptu soccer meet-up because one of our newest friends was really into soccer. I threw a quick, out-of-the-blue, unplanned text out to a smattering of folks I knew who were at least decent at the sport for a midweek game at the most inopportune time. And guess who was the first one to respond with a solid yes?

On the other hand, there was a woman who was the poster child of busy: she was a medical-surgical nurse, was doing a master's to become a nurse practitioner, needed to pick up extra shifts to make ends meet, and had hours that were clearly out of her control. She out of anyone could have easily said no to discipleship; she just did not have the time to do it. But she said yes, and whenever the discipleship core met, she guarded that time. Rain or shine, exhausted or not, she attended because she knew her presence mattered. On those occasions when a hospital shift or class or clinic was scheduled during the discipleship core meeting, she took ownership to reach out to me to meet up one-on-one to catch up. Despite her limited capacity, her vision for discipleship outweighed her lack of time.

Passion shapes priority, and believe it or not, capacity does not constitute calendar. Therefore we are left with the last category in the five Cs tool: confidence. Commitment has to do with clarity in vision and vision sets priority. Without clarity and specificity in vision, very few will make space and reorient their capacity (which has more to do with their passions than their calendar) for a new normal. And being discipled in the way of Jesus for the renewal of the community around us is the new normal.

VISION IS INVITATION

After John was put in prison, Jesus went into Galilee, proclaiming the good news of God. "The time has come," he said. "The kingdom of God has come near. Repent and believe the good news!"

As Jesus walked beside the Sea of Galilee, he saw Simon and his brother Andrew casting a net into the lake, for they were fishermen. "Come, follow me," Jesus said, "and I will send you out to fish for people." At once they left their nets and followed him.

When he had gone a little farther, he saw James son of Zebedee and his brother John in a boat, preparing their nets. Without delay he called them, and they left their father Zebedee in the boat with the hired men and followed him. (Mk 1:14-20)

Simon Peter, his brother Andrew, and James and John left everything and followed Jesus. They left their careers, their families and friends, and their hometowns in Galilee and followed Jesus. They left their expertise and what they were good at, their closest relationships, and the world they knew and followed Jesus. Vision helps people take ownership of their faith and commitment to God, and they need to be able to understand what it means to say yes to following Jesus. If you asked Peter or John why they followed Jesus, they wouldn't say, "Because Jesus died for me and saved me from my sins." Neither the crucifixion nor resurrection had happened yet. They didn't follow Jesus because of a message about salvation and earning a golden ticket to heaven and living the rest of your life twiddling your thumbs waiting for that ticket to be cashed in. And they didn't follow Jesus because he offered them a lucrative job, higher social status, or luxurious new destination. They followed Jesus because of two things and two things only: vision and the personal invitation into that vision.

Do you know why you follow Jesus? Would you be able to answer it without saying, "Because Jesus died for my sins"? Jesus absolutely did do that, but that's not it. It can't be it. The disciples followed Jesus because of the good news about something and because of Jesus' personal invitation into that something. The disciples followed Jesus because he told them the kingdom, the rule and reign, of God had come. And the disciples followed Jesus because he personally invited them. He painted a vision and invited them into it.

Dallas Willard calls the kingdom of God "the range of God's effective will."[10] Jesus' effective will reaches wherever his influence takes effect. In the kingdom of God everything is restored, peace and joy are beyond belief, goodness and prosperity mean every single person thrives—this was what was at hand and had come. And Jesus was personally offering it to his disciples. It had never been done before. The prophets of old had only told them what God had said to them. The kings of old had ruled them as poor stewards. The teachers, scribes, and Pharisees had only guided them on what they needed to do to follow God's instructions. But Jesus was saying that God would speak directly to them, directly rule them, and directly guide them. The kingdom of God at hand meant God was making himself directly and personally accessible to them.

Vision is the single most important thing the leader holds as they invite people into a shared life of discipleship, community, and mission. Without a clear and specific vision, invitation becomes vague, motivation is diluted, and availability becomes deprioritized.

Most church leaders do not spend nearly enough time setting clarity and specificity in vision, because it seems that the given vision for all of us in ministry is to "love God and love people." I mean, Jesus said himself that the greatest command was to live into the *Shema* (Deut 6:4-9) and extend it to those around us. But because of our current cultural context where faith has become both privatized and individualized, we as leaders need to clarify vision and specify what we hope for in our immediate, right-now, locally rooted contexts. We need a vision that clarifies what our communal love and commitment to God looks like and therefore specifies how that self-giving love will be present in the community around us.

If we live as though we follow Jesus only because he's died for our sins and we have a golden ticket to heaven, then life is just a waiting game. Waiting for retirement in heaven. Feeling safe about our own retirement plan and holding firmly to that ticket. Without a care in the world—we won the jackpot. there's really nothing left to do. But if we live as though we follow Jesus because his kingdom has come and he's personally invited us into a vibrant and vital relationship with him and into his kingdom, then there's a lot of life left to be lived. It's not a retirement plan; it's a reclaiming, restoration, and renovation plan. And a vision like that is quite alluring.

After Callie shared with me her hurdles—of having just started a new job, figuring out her new schedule, tending to the needs of her young children, and finding it difficult to even carve out time for her own marriage, we cried together. I shared with her my own struggles with having to juggle being a wife, mother, professional, community member, and friend. Then I asked her to recall specific stories with me. She recalled that she and her husband had some of their most meaningful conversations together during and after their times participating in our discipleship core and missional community; it had started to change their marriage. She recalled that her children loved having friends in our discipleship community and longed for more times like that. She recalled how much motivation and care she had personally experienced following Jesus in her own personal journey with him by being a part of a discipleship core.

At the end of that conversation, we clarified that the change that was needed was not to withdraw from the discipleship core; it was that she needed to ask the discipleship core if she and her husband could host it at their place every time.

Callie continues to host that discipleship core at her home today. Her husband participates just as much as she does, and her children's favorite people are members of that discipleship core.

12

DISCIPLESHIP IN CULTURE

*So where are we called to create culture? At the
intersection of grace and cross. Where do we find
our work and play bearing awe-inspiring fruit and
at the same time find ourselves able to identify with
Christ on the cross? That intersection is where we are
called to dig into the dirt, cultivate and create.*

ANDY CROUCH

*Then Agrippa said to Paul, "Do you think that in such
a short time you can persuade me to be a Christian?"
Paul replied, "Short time or long—I pray to God that
not only you but all who are listening to me today
may become what I am, except for these chains."*

ACTS 26:28-29

IN *THE RISE OF CHRISTIANITY*, sociologist Rodney Stark looks at
what Jesus' followers committed to do and be in the time of the plagues
of Rome in AD 165 and 251.[1] Life in the city at that time was one of
"disease, misery, and fear." But it provided a way for those committed to
Jesus to commit themselves to one another and to the culture around
them. Their presence mattered deeply. They chose to believe in the
presence of God, be more present with one another, and be present in

the community and culture around them. They imagined a better world in the coming future but also were present in the solutions for present-day concerns and uncertainties. They so served and loved the community and culture around them that this simple act of self-giving love while the rest of the city fled and left the most vulnerable behind—their act of presence—was an apologetic for the world around them in a way that made nations look at the power of the cross. Jesus invites the church to movement, not mere establishment. He moves us to partner with him in deep communion, flourishing community, and transformative mission. He calls his disciples to follow him into a communal life of self-giving love for the sake of the gospel of the kingdom of God for a postmodern world that desperately needs to root its belonging and purpose in Christ.

DISCIPLESHIP WITHIN CULTURE MATTERS

We've been looking at the need to radically change our job description as church leaders to mature missional disciplemakers and restructuring our churches, moving discipleship from the periphery to the center. What happens, then, to a group of disciples who are growing in maturity in Christlike character, theology, wisdom, and missional living? What kind of effect does a group of people who are imitating Jesus have on the culture and community around them?

They begin to change it.

Their presence begins to matter in their neighborhoods and social networks. A transformation begins to take place in the extended community's identity, purpose, justice, sense of belonging, wholeness, truth, and beauty. An inexplicable goodness begins to be cultivated, and a culture of self-giving love, imitating Jesus' love for us and the whole world, begins to be established. Discipleship doesn't just affect the person or group being discipled; it extends out into all the cultural spheres of life the disciple moves in and out of.

If we look at how Scripture paints a picture of the church, we see that the church has always been God's people engaging in the cultural spheres of life. The original word for "church" is the Greek word *ekklēsia*, which at its heart means "the people of God who are sent out." The church is made up of people who belong to God and are called to go out and advance his kingdom's presence; it is not a well-intentioned, well-meaning social club that gathers more and more people into its well-managed programs and activities. The church is about multiplying mature missional disciples— not spectators—and sending them out into the local culture they are rooted in.

SEVEN CULTURAL SPHERES OF LIFE

If we were to tally what Jesus talked most about, we would see that his conversations were oriented around one thing: the kingdom of God. He connected the Son of Man to the kingdom of God and described what the kingdom of God is like. And he told parable after parable about how the kingdom of God is worth it. It's worth it to invest our time, talent (skills, gifts, etc.), and treasure (resources, finances, networks, etc.). And Jesus talked much about how the kingdom of God influences its surrounding culture.

When we think of culture today and what areas influence it the most, we can boil it down to these seven spheres (listed in no particular order of importance):[2]

- Government
- Arts and entertainment
- Education
- Family
- Media
- Business
- Church (institutionalized religion)

These seven cultural spheres of life are the essential, shaped, and molded pieces of society that speak to the way in which not just individuals but large cohorts of people do life. These arenas of culture influence and dictate how people see, think, feel, and do life. Our aim in making mature missional disciples is to influence the very spaces that most influence society.

In considering these seven spheres of life that influence how communities and cultures operate, we can ask the following questions:

- Why these particular seven cultural spheres?
- What if I'm not involved in any of these cultural spheres?
- What if the cultural sphere I do participate in isn't included in these seven?

Literature in the fields of philosophy, sociology, anthropology, and psychology all conclude that these spheres are the major influencers in a culture. We can pretty much take anything that seems separate from these seven spheres and see how it fits into at least one of these spaces. They are "the various dimensions of life that come together to make up society as we know it."[3]

Many people in the field of medicine (myself included) or charity/cause-related organizations find themselves asking, Why isn't there a separate arena for us? Let's take medicine, for example. If we're trying to impregnate these seven cultural spheres with the kingdom of God and drive out the lies the enemy is using to influence how people see and do life, then medicine is involved in two ways. One, medicine is already an industry that works to heal, restore, and bring health to people. Its very nature is already aligned with the kingdom of God in a way that seeks to reclaim his people to its original intent. Two, in the aspects of medicine where we don't see Jesus' full reign here on earth, it's less about the act of participating in healing than it is about the culture that acts on it. Meaning this: if there's something off about how the field of medicine views the human body, something that isn't aligned with how God thinks about us, it has more to do with the cultural sphere of education than with medicine itself. If there's something off about how the field of medicine provides access to healthcare for people, it has more to do with the cultural sphere of government than medicine itself. If there's something off about how a certain hospital or clinic functions, it has more to do with the cultural sphere of business than medicine itself. The influencing potential doesn't reside within the field of medicine; it lies within one of the seven spheres of culture. When physicians in the Nazi regime were allowed to practice horrendous acts on Jews, these acts weren't carried out through the field of medicine; they were done at the behest of the government under the guise of education.

Let's look at charitable organizations. Again, most charities, nonprofits, environmental groups, and human rights organizations are already aligned with the work of the kingdom of God as it seeks to reclaim his people and creation. But, again, the results that begin to influence culture come about through the seven cultural spheres of life. The best human rights activist groups rely on three branches of work to accomplish their goals: one, influencing the government by lobbying and networking, two, raising awareness via education and media to change thought processes, and three, raising support via the major social and economic influencers in culture: arts and entertainment and business.

The question, then, isn't about why a particular occupation, passion, or calling doesn't fit into the seven spheres; it's about how that amalgamation can effect change and bring the kingdom of God to the world via the seven arenas. And if we dissect each arena to see how it influences culture and what strongholds it has over culture, we can see the venues in which we should participate in order to bring the good news of the kingdom of God. While not an exhaustive list (and I'm leaving out the cultural sphere of institutionalized religion), table 12.1 depicts how each cultural sphere sets values for society and also its unique stronghold that is at odds with the culture of the kingdom of Jesus.

Table 12.1. Cultural spheres of influence set cultural values

Cultural arena	Cultural influence	Cultural value
Families	**Sets:** Values, defines your "people" **Stronghold:** Selfishness, "us" versus "other"	Belonging
Education	**Sets:** How to think and what to think about **Stronghold:** Selfishness, "us" versus "other"	Truth
Arts and Entertainment	**Sets:** Cultural narrative and beauty **Stronghold:** Distorted images of self, success, power	Beauty
Government and Politics	**Sets:** Morality and law **Stronghold:** Gaining, ruling over others, exploitation	Justice
Media	**Sets:** Community and current events **Stronghold:** What to have eyes on (low celebration/trust, high anxiety/suspicion)	Story
Business	**Sets:** Economy and wealth **Stronghold:** Love of money, status	Worth

Most Christians think the role of the church is to be at the center of culture. Investing in God's kingdom is synonymous with making more church programs. Interacting with the culture looks like bringing everyone from every part of culture to church so they also can participate in these programs and activities. The businessperson becomes part of the church board. The educator helps out with children's ministry. The musician joins the worship team.

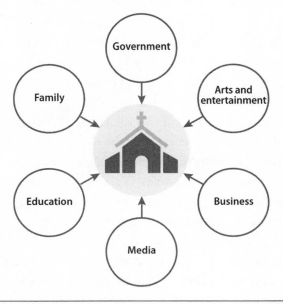

Figure 12.1. Church as center of culture: When the church is at the center, then we utilize the cultural spheres of influence to serve the structure and maintenance of the church.

But what if that is the wrong direction? And what if the institution of church is just one of the arenas of culture? If the church doesn't belong in the center of influence, what does?

The goal isn't to put the institution of church at the center of everything; it's to put Jesus at the center of everything. I'll go one step further: when I say "Jesus," I'm not just putting the Jesus who died on the cross at the center. No, I'm putting King Jesus at the center. This life doesn't end with an assurance that we are saved through Jesus and life becomes a waiting game. No, when the kingdom of God comes, it's King Jesus at the helm, and it changes everything. Every aspect of society now. People will begin to do family differently. Education will begin to be transformed; businesses will begin to look at more than just the bottom line.

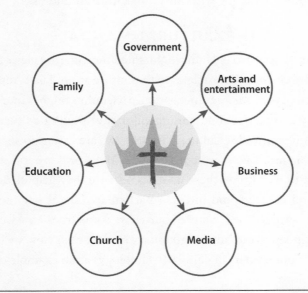

Figure 12.2. King Jesus as the center of culture: When Jesus is at the center, then we partner with him in moving into the cultural spheres of influence. It also moves "church" from the center to one of the cultural arenas that Jesus is transforming and redeeming.

The incredible truth is that King Jesus is already doing this. In his inauguration, Jesus proclaimed, "The time is fulfilled, and the kingdom of God is at hand; repent and believe in the gospel" (Mk 1:15 ESV). He's already transforming and restoring culture, and his favorite way to do this is through his people. People just like you and me. He puts all of us in different cultural spheres of life, and he gives us time, talents, and treasure so we will go and advance his kingdom right where we're at.

A discipleship pathway doesn't stop at helping an individual take a good hard look at their own life; it helps move a group of people to start thinking about their shared community, their neighborhoods and networks, the very places where the kingdom of God is already actively working to renew and transform for the flourishing of everyone. A discipleship pathway is both formational and missional—when a group of people journey together to imitate Jesus, they are sent out for the sake of others. The direction is outward, not inward. Discipleship, a community maturing into the likeness of Jesus in his character, theology, wisdom, and missional living, requires engaging and interacting with the local culture around us.

THE CULTURAL MANDATE

Theologian H. Richard Niebuhr highlighted the differing views that Christians hold about how Jesus relates to the culture around us.[4] Andy Crouch, in his book *Culture Making*, incorporates Niebuhr's themes into these contemporary categories: condemning culture, critiquing culture, copying culture, and consuming culture.[5] These views are meant to shed light on the often nuanced ways we participate in the world around us, and it's important to pick up on these nuances because they help us understand background contexts and intents—particularly about our identity and purpose. As we will see, many of our views come from how we think we need to respond to the culture around us. And for each view, we'll also look at a contemporary part of culture (technology) as an example of how the view functions.

Christ against culture (condemning culture). Most of us who have been immersed in Christian culture and Christianese are conformed to the idea that all the world around us is broken. In fact it is, but we're led to believe that because it's broken, it's inherently evil. There's a suspicion against the culture of the world because of its sinfulness and a feeling that we shouldn't have anything to do with it. So we seclude ourselves from culture and don't participate in it. When I'm presented with a new technology, I don't buy it. Literally. I won't engage with it at all because of my view that all technology is inherently evil.

Christ of culture (copying culture). Syncretism results from the perspective that we can't do anything about the culture around us, so if we can't beat them, join them. In this view a follower of Jesus has no comment or constructive criticism concerning the culture but instead fully participates in it without exerting any influence over it. One wouldn't be able to tell the difference between the culture in the church and the culture in the world, no difference between a follower of Jesus and a non-follower of Jesus. So when I'm presented with a new technology, I'm absolutely going to purchase it for my own advantage, without a thought for any of the consequences it may have in my life.

Christ above culture (critiquing culture). In this view the follower of Jesus engages with the surrounding culture by making all of culture highlight or include Christ. All art, all retail, all business, all technology—every single aspect of the culture needs to be about Jesus. Its people only make artwork that features Jesus, all apps are Christian apps, all education is Christian education, and we only patronize Christian businesses.

Christ in culture (consuming culture). While the previous view is a moderate version of suspicion, this one is the moderate version of syncretism. It tells the Christian to be in the world but not of the world—we live in parallel with the culture, experiencing a constant tension with the culture. When presented with a new technology, we'll consider each aspect of it and take precautions to know if we can engage with that particular aspect or not. We can't beat the culture, but we can pick and choose which parts to join and not join.

Table 12.2. Understanding Christ and culture shapes how discipleship engages with culture

	How do we feel about culture?	How do we respond to culture?
Christ against culture (condemning culture)	Suspicion	Seclusion
Christ of culture (copying culture)	Syncretism	Full permission + participation
Christ above culture (critiquing culture)	Suspicion with participation	Change all of it to be Christian
Christ in culture (consuming culture)	Syncretism with caution	Live in parallel
Christ transforming culture (making culture)	Sacrificial love	Redeem and create it

Christ transforming culture. Each of the differing perspectives, while understandable in its respective reasoning, comes from a point of view where the disciple of Jesus doesn't understand their role in the culture. They don't understand the role of the people of God *for* the culture. That role is to fully participate and engage with the culture around them in order to extend the rule and reign of Jesus into every aspect of culture for two reasons: to glorify God and to allow all those around them to flourish. How do we feel about the culture? Sacrificial love. How do we respond to the culture? Redeem and create it. Crouch states:

> Culture making is needed in every company, every school and every church. In every place there are impossibilities that leave even the powerful feeling constrained and drained, and that rob the powerless of the ability to imagine something different and better. At root, every human cultural enterprise is haunted by the ultimate impossibility, death, which threatens to slam shut the door of human hope. But God is at work precisely in these places where the impossible seems absolute. Our calling is to join him in what he is already doing—to make visible what, in exodus and resurrection, he has already done.[6]

Simply put, discipleship (and using a discipleship pathway) helps people answer these two key questions: "Who am I?" and "What I am supposed to do?" The imitation of Jesus into incarnational love for others answers the call for both identity and purpose. And a discipleship pathway helps disciples to reconnect to the cultural mandate.

What do I mean by the cultural mandate?[7] We see in Genesis 1 that when God created human beings, he gave them a specific identity and a specific purpose:

> So God created man in his own image, in the image of God he created him; male and female he created them. And God blessed them. And God said to them, "Be fruitful and multiply and fill the earth and subdue it, and have dominion over the fish of the sea and over the birds of the heavens and over every living thing that moves on the earth." (Gen 1:27-28)

Our identity is set in being made in God's image—we are his image-bearers. Our purpose is to be fruitful and have dominion—we are his representatives.

The problem is that we often limit our view of this mandate, believing God wants us only to have children and take care of the earth. Have a family and work. That's what we uniquely do as God's image-bearers. But if that's the extent of God's original intent for us, one, it excludes those who can't fulfill it (be married or bear children), and two, it doesn't sound all that worthwhile—sort of like, "Keep to yourself and take care of your own." But our identity and purpose extend far beyond this limited view. Because we are God's image-bearers, our cultural mandate is to create culture. We create culture because we imitate God. We do this in two distinct ways: by developing the social world, network, and framework around us and by harnessing the natural world in a way that something emerges that allows the human heart to flourish—in other words, to organize and release the potential of the raw elements in a way that reflects the very image of God. Culture makers.

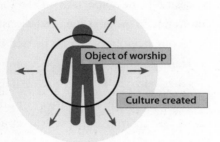

Figure 12.3. Relationship between worship and culture

And because we are all created in God's image and given the purpose to create culture around us, all of us do this. It's our cultural mandate. We create social constructs around us and we create culture around us, in one shape or another. Our ability and capability do not depend on whether we acknowledge or are even aware of God. We wouldn't say a certain person does not bear the image of God just because they don't know God. The thing about culture is that because we are by default culture makers, it's inevitable that we will build culture around us—we can't help but do this. Every single one of us. The only difference is what we actually cultivate. In essence, culture is the expression of the thing we hold most valuable, most beautiful, most important. Simply put, we worship what we orient culture around.

We can clearly see what is esteemed above everything else by looking at any given culture. Culture can glorify God or it can dash him to the ground. It can allow everyone to flourish or it can segregate and deem some as

worthy and others obsolete. It can contribute to people reaching their potential or it can bring destruction on humanity. We know instantly when
money is in the center of our affection because the culture we build around
it reflects that. We know when an idealized body type is the most desirable
thing because the culture elevates appearance as supreme. We know when
we worship a certain way of doing family life because how we create culture
will display it.

Money, physical beauty, and relationships are not evil things. They're
actually very good things. But when any of them is worshiped—deemed
as the most valuable, desirable, or important—then the culture will be
built around it. If it's money, then social culture, relationships, friendships,
and how we engage with our neighbors will all be tied to finances. We'll
associate only with certain people of a certain economic status. We'll
engage only in activities that help our bottom line. We'll make all decisions
and spend our time and resources only to improve our financial gain. And
because of how we create culture, our purpose is wrapped tightly to our
identity. All of a sudden, money has the final say in who we are. If we don't
have it, we're not valuable. If we don't have it, we're not loved.

Let's take something that's depicted as inherently good—family life. The
most wholesome and life-giving family you can imagine—spouse of your
dreams, two kids, dog, white picket fence, the whole lot. Nothing bad about
it. But when family is the thing that takes the worship seat, again, culture
grows around it. All social networking will revolve around bettering our
family alone. We will play an inclusion and exclusion game to determine
which social engagements will make our family thrive—which play dates
with which other children will better our child's social welfare and not
threaten our family. Decisions about where to live, what job to choose, what
extracurriculars our child will be involved in, what to spend money on—all
of this will be determined solely to maintain that ideal family picture. And
what's worse is that, if any of these things were to be skewed—the not-ideal
spouse and you start having tension in your marriage; you find out one of
the not-ideal children has a learning disability; you discover you can no
longer afford to live in the not-ideal family home—these things will begin
to unmake you as a person. Why? Because you worshiped family.

The good and bad part of what you worship isn't the point—the point is that the worship seat of each of us, and therefore the worship seat of every culture, is meant to be God. As his image-bearers, we are meant to create culture around the worship of God in a way that glorifies him and establishes the flourishing of all people.

So how does any of this relate to the viewpoint of Christ transforming culture? Well, it has everything to do with it.

CULTURE TRANSFORMED

Because we can't help but create culture around us, who and what we worship matters. It determines how and why we make decisions. It determines what we invest our resources and time and energy into. It affects who we associate ourselves with and engage in conversation. You see, because we can't help but create culture, we'll do it in a manner that reflects what's at the center of our worship. And having God at the center of our worship, as individuals and as a collective of people, means we begin to create culture in a way that reflects who God is: his nature of community and grace and truth, his loves and his hates, his heart for renewal and reclaiming through the way of sacrifice.

Because we can't help but create culture, we'll establish or participate in social networks by default. We can't help but form and shape families, neighborhoods, teams, cities and towns, schools, social clubs, parties, and friendships. And when creating these social frameworks is aligned with God and his heart and very nature, we begin to create families and friendships in a way that he does. Imagine a neighborhood where Jesus' influence is supreme and we deem one another's safety and well-being more important than our own. Or we plan parties in a way that is inviting and hospitable to the disenfranchised in the community because Jesus constantly noticed and welcomed the marginalized.

Betsy would say she's not any good at most anything except cooking. She makes sure there's a pot of chili cooking on the stove in case an unexpected guest arrives. When I was asking her to share about how the kingdom of God was coming into her personal world, she just sort of shrugged her shoulder and dismissed it, saying it wasn't a big deal.

"What do you mean?"

"Oh, we make sure to have our home open for folks from the mainland who can't really afford travel unless they have a place to stay. And most of these people are friends and families we've known for years who don't really know Jesus, so we're their best connection to him. I stay up past my bedtime to have faith conversations with them—we just make ourselves available to have honest conversations."

What Betsy is failing to mention is that she's allowing herself—her time and energy and resources—to be inconvenienced by visitors because she wants to create a safe place for people to have honest conversations about their spiritual life. She is creating a social framework.

"It's not much, but I love the girls in this [at-risk teen pregnancy center], and I volunteer to drive them to their meeting space. Then once I'm there, I love to be in the background and help make crafts with them. You know, whatever they need."

She waves her hand and rolls her eyes as if she were shooing herself off. But Betsy is not this silent-as-a-mouse kind of person—she has a warm, loving, huge personality where people instantly fall in love with her. When she's driving those young women, she's not just silently driving; she's asking questions about their lives, and people always seem to spill their guts to Betsy. Likewise, making crafts doesn't mean she's just cutting away at paper; she's fully engaged and listening to every girl's life story and also being vulnerable and sharing her own painful stories, all the while unashamedly weaving Jesus into her stories. And not in a way that's cumbersome but with the perfect mix of dialogue—the kind where there's a true exchange of stories. Betsy's a whiz at creating a social framework where people feel valued.

I watched her get a little shy. "What?" I asked.

"Well, again, it's nothing big, but we try to have our neighbors over for dinner once a month, just so we get to know all of them—I mean, we all live in the same place! And we're gonna try to get a permit from the city to block off our cul-de-sac and do a big block party! Won't that be fun! So it's not just us getting to know our neighbors but everyone. I pray Jesus will show up and give us opportunities to share with them."

I know many people who say they're asking the Lord for opportunities to talk to people about Jesus but don't follow through when the opportunity presents itself. When Betsy says this, she means every word of it. A neighborhood block party in the hopes it will glorify God and establish the flourishing of the people around her.

Creating culture.

ORGANIZING THE RAW INTO THE COMPLEX

Having dominion over the whole earth is basically taking the raw elements of creation and transforming them into something organized and purposeful. You can see this in any element of society. Music takes the raw materials of sound and organizes and develops them in a way that creates a beautiful song. A book takes the raw materials of words and phrases and pieces them together in a way that arrives at *War and Peace.* Education collects the raw materials of thoughts and facts and orders them in a system by which to message and learn. Law harnesses the raw materials of ideas of morality and transforms them into a code of ethics to bring order to society. We could go on and on. Economy. Government. Painting. Film.

What happens when our worship of God starts to affect how we harness raw materials and transform them into something complex? What happens when glorifying God and establishing the flourishing of all people affect the way in which we create financial systems, make movies, write songs, or run our businesses? Let's look at business more closely. When God aligns us to what's important to him and what he loves, our plans for leadership (valuing integrity and generosity), strategy (making products and services geared to renew culture and not exploit it), and operations (managing our company in a way that invests back into the community it's located in and into the lives of employees) all fall in line with him. Or if we write a love song, we produce music not so it tops the chart or oversexualizes relationships, but rather we write about how God thinks and feels about love and how he dignifies people.

There's a craft-beer-tasting room in my neighborhood, and I remember the first time I walked into that establishment. It had just opened up a week earlier and featured industrial decor, plain walls, and plastic crates for seats—it was definitely just starting up. After getting a four-ounce taster, I sat and looked around. For wall decor, there were a couple of photographs printed on metal: two profile pictures of children from developing countries and another photo of a laundromat. Interesting, to say the least. It intrigued me enough to strike up a conversation with the woman behind the register.

Turns out Holly and her husband, Tim, are business culture makers in the kingdom of God. Their beer tasting joint, Grace in Growlers, donates all profits to organizations that seek to lift people out of poverty. They used to live the dream life in SoCal, traveling to exotic places around the world, enjoying the best that life can offer. And they attended one of the largest established churches in the country. But they stopped and said, "This isn't how life is supposed to work. Something's wrong. We're not living like we're a part of Jesus' kingdom."

So they left everything they knew, moved to a small town in Hawaii, opened up a craft beer place, and now work seven days a week to make money they're not ever going to use on themselves. They're giving it all away because they were struck by Jesus' compassion for those in need. And if you're working seven days a week, guess what you can't do anymore? No more traveling to exotic places. No more living it up and acquiring all the luxuries life offers. Instead they give generously to Compassion International, and in what little free time they have, they frequent a local laundromat, getting to know the houseless population there and allowing that community to have clean clothes for free.

DISCIPLEMAKERS AND CULTURE MAKERS

If Jesus is at the center, then discipleship is also at the center, because discipleship is simply imitating Christ and maturing into Christlike character, theology, wisdom, and missional living. The sent people of God offer to all people "a vision of the goal of human history in which its good is affirmed and its evil is forgiven and taken away, a vision which makes it possible to act hopefully when there is no earthly hope."[8] Discipleship utilizing a discipleship pathway not only makes disciplemakers but also culture makers.

If we as leaders are constantly revisiting Dallas Willard's questions, "Do you have a plan for discipleship? And is your plan working?" then discipleship will become central to the life of our church and communities. When discipleship becomes central, we are forming disciplemakers who are making more disciplemakers and culture makers who are renewing the culture around them.

EPILOGUE

JESUS INTENDS FOR DISCIPLES to make disciples in the context of community. Jesus intends for disciples to make disciples in the context of a community on mission together. A discipleship pathway led by mature disciples who are concrete models of a life worth imitating equips a committed group of people in the ways of Jesus for the sake of the neighborhoods and networks around them. The assumption that discipleship happens best in a private, one-on-one manner is a misnomer provided by the Western postmodern belief that religion should be privatized and individualized. This couldn't be further from the truth. Jesus made disciples and commissioned his disciples to go and make disciples through the beauty of community—a community that has set out to renew culture and announce the life-giving reign and rule of God.

I started in the prologue with a snapshot of what happened to my church, *Ma Ke Alo o*, in March of 2020 because of centering discipleship. I'll close with a letter I wrote to the disciples in my church at the end of 2021:

> I was recently invited to be the keynote speaker for a network of churches of predominantly minority (Black and Brown) leaders. They were early mornings given that it was a virtual conference, with about 300 people, leaders of communities that have been in existence for decades, those that are persevering through the first years and those that will soon be vibrant and full of hope in their own unique neighborhoods and locally rooted places. We sat together in a variety of ways in a variety of virtual rooms, processing and learning and being equipped in how to be present with one another and present in the community we live in.

I met a Caucasian man who just started a church in his sixties because he had a heart for the autistic community in his neighborhood—he was honestly one of the most joyful people I have ever met. I met a *hapa* Black woman who is a social worker by trade, recently had a baby, finds rest in hosting celebrations, and is passionate about starting a community on mission together but didn't know if she was the right kind of leader. I met a Hispanic woman who was translating all of my talks into Spanish. I met a Black man, the national director of this network, who was patient and kind even in the midst of having such a difficult year being confronted with racism at a new level.

I got to experience all of this recently because of you.

I was invited to be the keynote speaker at this conference because they needed someone to equip them in discipleship. Discipleship that moves a community into mission together. They needed someone to talk to them about how living together (community) in the way of Jesus (communion) for the renewal of the culture around us (co-mission) is what changes neighborhoods and networks and reshapes community and culture.

They needed someone to talk to them about *Ma Ke Alo o*.

It was a joy and a privilege to talk story with these people, representing many different people groups, about how vital discipleship is. And not just discipleship as a way of learning something new, but embedded into a community of people who are intentionally walking this life together. Jesus banked his whole claim of new life and the goodness of the kingdom of God on how a community of people chooses to love one another for the sake of the world.

We started our year together sitting in how we demonstrate Jesus' love to the culture and community around us through the way we love one another. In each of our missional communities. In each of our unique discipleship cores. As we turn the corner, my hope is that I too bank on the same thing Jesus did—on community, being formed in the profound and beautiful ways of Jesus, living for the renewal of our beloved Hawaiian Islands.

My continued hope even now is to bank on the same thing Jesus did—on centering discipleship in all of our churches and communities. Centering discipleship where people become formed in the profound and beautiful ways of Jesus and live together for the renewal of our cities, communities, and culture.

ACKNOWLEDGMENTS

THEY SAY IT TAKES EXPERTISE and good penmanship to write a book. On the contrary, I've learned that it takes experience and friendship to write one—especially a book on discipleship. Jesus banked on forming core experiences and friendship to ignite discipleship, not on know-how or skills.

I've learned that experiences, both those that are indescribably painful and equally inspirational, help me to have something to write about.

I've learned, more importantly, that friendship helps to keep this written contribution accessible, relatable, and meaningful.

To my *Ma Ke Alo o 'ohana*, where would I be without you? You are entirely my muse, and without you, this book wouldn't exist. Hanzo and Meli, Ed and Mark, you live lives worth imitating. Kelci and Paige, Keven, Melissa and Gabe, Mars, Haku, Callie, Timmy and Thaisa, Roz and Craig, Laine, Timmy, and Holly, you build communities worth inviting into. This whole book could have been filled with stories upon stories about each of you. I would run out of pages.

To my V3 family, where would I have found my voice? You have been a mirror for me, reflecting back who I am, where I'm running, and who I get to run with. Josh, I have never met a pastor quite like you; I live only a fraction of the life of self-giving love you lead. Cory, if you didn't exist, I don't think a church like mine could ever fit in. Kyuboem, you have been my hero since I first met Jesus and still are. JR, if the Holy Spirit didn't connect us, I would have been lost. Taeler, no one else taught me the importance of keeping vision, leadership, and discipleship central. Ben, I wouldn't have pared down discipleship to increasing spiritual confidence and social competence without your wisdom. I imitate each of you as you each imitate Jesus.

To Al Hsu, my editor, your guidance (and far better word choices) has been paramount for a first-time author, but more than that, it has been your remarkable kindness and clarity in your own writing that have paved the way for people like me.

To my children, Beren, Emma, and Kyriella, you are my hope. I have credibility and gravitas in who I am, what I write, and how I live only because of each of you. My heart.

To my husband, Steve, if every person were to follow you in the ways you love Jesus and love others, then this book would be utterly obsolete. My own formation and discipleship are profoundly indebted to yours.

NOTES

PROLOGUE

[1]Andy Crouch, Kurt Keilhacker, and Dave Blanchard, "Leading Beyond the Blizzard: Why Every Organization is Now a Startup," *The Praxis Journal*, March 20, 2020, http://journal.praxislabs.org/leading-beyond-the-blizzard-why-every-organization-is-now-a-startup-b7f32fb278ff.

[2]Crouch, Keilhacker, and Blanchard, "Leading Beyond the Blizzard."

[3]Aaron Earls, "Protestant Church Closures Outpace Openings in U.S.," Lifeway Research, May 25, 2021, https://research.lifeway.com/2021/05/25/protestant-church-closures-outpace-openings-in-u-s.

[4]Aaron Earls, "More Churches Closed than Opened in 2019. Then Came the Pandemic," *Christianity Today*, May 25, 2021, www.christianitytoday.com/news/2021/may/lifeway-church-close-open-2019-planting-revitalization.html.

[5]Ministry Brands, "Ministry Brands Releases Survey Data Revealing the Role of Technology in the Church During the Pandemic and Beyond," PR Newswire, August 10, 2021, www.prnewswire.com/news-releases/ministry-brands-releases-survey-data-revealing-the-role-of-technology-in-the-church-during-the-pandemic-and-beyond-301352679.html.

[6]Tony Morgan, "New Data on How Churches Are Responding to the Pandemic Today: Episode 148," *The Unstuck Church Podcast*, www.theunstuckgroup.com/church-survey-data-coronavirus-crisis-episode-148-unstuck-church-podcast.

1. MAKING DISCIPLESHIP CENTRAL

[1]Brandi Watkins, *Research Perspectives on Social Media Influencers and Their Followers* (Washington, DC: Lexington Books, 2021), 235.

[2]See Mt 4:19; 16:24; 19:28; Mk 1:17; 10:21; Lk 5:27; Jn 1:38; 8:12; 21:19.

[3]"Disciples," New Catholic Encyclopedia, Encyclopedia.com, October 21, 2022, www.encyclopedia.com/religion/encyclopedias-almanacs-transcripts-and-maps/disciples.

[4]1 Cor 4:16; 11:1; Eph 5:1; 1 Thess 1:6; 2:14; Heb 6:12; 1 Pet 3:13.

[5]Murray Harris, *Navigating Tough Texts: A Guide to Problem Passages in the New Testament* (Bellingham, WA: Lexham Press, 2020), 24.

[6]James Wellman, Katie E. Corcoran, and Kate Stockly-Meyerdirk, "'God Is Like a Drug': Explaining Interaction Ritual Chains in American Megachurches," *Sociological Forum* 29, no. 3 (September 2014): 650-72. Of note: 470 interviews and 16,000 surveys were conducted.

[7]See Mt 7:28; 13:54; 19:25; 22:33; Mk 1:22; 6:2; 7:37; 10:26; Lk 4:32; 5:9; 8:56; 9:43; Jn 6:66.

[8]JR Woodward, "Public Space: From Idolizing or Demonizing to Re-imagining" (The V3 Movement, June 2020). Also note key concepts from Karl Vaters, "Jesus and Crowds— An Unhappy Marriage," *Christianity Today*, June 28, 2017, www.christianitytoday.com /karl-vaters/2017/june/jesus-and-crowds-unhappy-marriage.html; and Graham Tomlin, *The Provocative Church* (London: SPCK and Sheldon Press, 2014).

2. THE NATURE OF DISCIPLESHIP

[1]Ben Lutkevich, "Definition Framework," TechTarget, WhatIs.com, August 2020, www .techtarget.com/whatis/definition/framework.

[2]Lesslie Newbigin, *The Gospel in a Pluralist Society* (Grand Rapids, MI: Eerdmans, 1989), chap. 19, Kindle.

[3]David Bosch, *Transforming Mission: Paradigm Shifts in Theology of Mission* (Maryknoll, NY: Orbis Books, 1991), 335.

[4]Christine Pohl, *Living into Community: Cultivating Practices that Sustain Us* (Grand Rapids, MI: Eerdmans, 2012), chap. 1, Kindle.

[5]Neil Cole, *Ordinary Hero: Becoming a Disciple Who Makes a Difference* (Grand Rapids, MI: Baker Books, 2008), 185.

[6]JR Woodward, "Multiplying Disciples Through the Four Spaces of Belonging" (The V3 Movement article, 2020), 7.

[7]Philip R. Meadows, "Wesleyan Wisdom for Mission-Shaped Discipleship," *Journal of Missional Practice* 3, January 2014.

3. THE MARKS OF A MATURE DISCIPLE

[1]Greg McKinzie, "An Abbreviated Introduction to the Concept of *Missio Dei*," *Missio Dei Journal* 1 (August 2010): http://missiodeijournal.com/issues/md-1/authors/md-1 -mckinzie.

[2]Michael Kinnamon and Brian E. Cope, *The Ecumenical Movement: An Anthology of Key Texts and Voices* (Grand Rapids, MI: Eerdmans, 1997), 339-40.

[3]David J. Bosch, *Transforming Mission: Paradigm Shifts in Theology of Mission,* American Society of Missiology Series 16 (Maryknoll, NY: Orbis, 1991), 393, 512.

[4]Dan White Jr., "5 Steps for Creating a Discipleship Pathway," V3, thev3movement. org/2018/03/21/5-steps-for-creating-a-discipleship-pathway. Accessed November 18, 2022.

[5] Adapted from JR Woodward and Dan White Jr., *The Church as Movement: Starting and Sustaining Missional-Incarnational Communities* (Downers Grove, IL: InterVarsity Press, 2016), chap. 4, Kindle.

[6] Tim Keller, "Proverbs: True Wisdom for Living," sermon series, Redeemer Presbyterian Church, New York, September 2004.

[7] Tormod Engelsviken, "Missio Dei: The Understanding and Misunderstanding of a Theological Concept in European Churches and Missiology," *International Review of Mission* 92, no. 367 (October 2003): 482.

[8] Lesslie Newbigin, *A Word in Season: Perspectives on Christian World Missions* (Grand Rapids, MI: Eerdmans, 1994), 150.

[9] Woodward, "Multiplying Disciples Through the Four Spaces of Belonging."

[10] Adapted from JR Woodward, *Creating a Missional Culture: Equipping the Church for the Sake of the World* (Downers Grove, IL: InterVarsity Press, 2012), 121.

[11] Woodward and White, *Church as Movement*, 146.

[12] Deb Hirsch, "Community Life," teaching session, Praxis Gathering, Philadelphia, 2019.

[13] Jonathan Brooks, "Sometimes the Church Needs to Follow and Partner with Others," Faith & Leadership, June 26, 2018, www.faithandleadership.com/jonathan-brooks -sometimes-the-church-needs-follow-and-partner-others.

4. FROM PAST RECIPES TO LOCAL CUISINE

[1] Barna, "Signs of Decline and Hope Among Key Metrics of Faith," Barna: State of the Church 2020, March 4, 2020, www.barna.com/research/changing-state-of-the -church.

[2] Tim Keller, *Center Church: Doing Balanced, Gospel-Centered Ministry in Your City* (Grand Rapids, MI: Zondervan, 2012), chap. 15, Kindle.

[3] Isabel Wilkerson, *Caste: The Origins of Our Discontents* (New York: Random House, 2020), chap. 6, Kindle.

5. ESSENTIAL INGREDIENTS FOR ANY PATHWAY

[1] See Søren Kierkegaard, *Practice in Christianity* (Princeton, NJ: Princeton Paperbacks, 1991).

[2] Christine D. Pohl, *Living into Community* (Grand Rapids, MI: Eerdmans, 2012), chap. 1, Kindle.

[3] Adapted from JR Woodward and Dan White Jr., *The Church as Movement: Starting and Sustaining Missional-Incarnational Communities* (Downers Grove, IL: InterVarsity Press, 2016), chap. 7, Kindle.

[4] Dallas Willard, *The Divine Conspiracy: Rediscovering Our Hidden Life in God* (Chicago: Harper Collins, 1998), 21.

[5] Lesslie Newbigin, *Sign of the Kingdom* (Grand Rapids, MI. Eerdmans, 1980).

6. THE JOURNEY OF A DISCIPLESHIP PATHWAY

[1]Benedict Atkins, personal correspondence with author, September 27, 2021.

7. DISCIPLESHIP REQUIRES TRANSFORMATION

[1]Marcia Daszko and Sheila Sheinberg, "Survival Is Optional: Only Leaders with New Knowledge Can Pivot, Disrupt, & Lead a Transformation," LinkedIn, October 18, 2021, www.linkedin.com/pulse/survival-optional-only-leaders-new-knowledge-can -pivot-marcia-daszko.

[2]Carol H. Weiss, "Theory-Based Evaluation: Theories of Change for Poverty Reduction Programs," in *Evaluation and Poverty Reduction: Proceedings from a World Bank Conference*, ed. Osvaldo Feinstein and Robert Picciotto (Washington, DC: International Bank for Reconstruction and Development, 2000), 103.

8. UNMASKING OUR DISCIPLESHIP ASSUMPTIONS

[1]Carol H. Weiss, "Theory-Based Evaluation: Theories of Change for Poverty Reduction Programs," in *Evaluation and Poverty Reduction: Proceedings from a World Bank Conference*, ed. Osvaldo Feinstein and Robert Picciotto (Washington, DC: International Bank for Reconstruction and Development, 2000), 103.

[2]Jay Kim, "How to Church Shop Like the First Christians," *Christianity Today*, January 20, 2022, www.christianitytoday.com/ct/2022/january-web-only/covid-church -hopping-shopping-new-year-trend.html.

[3]Dietrich Bonhoeffer, *Life Together: The Classic Exploration of Christian Community*, (London: SCM Press Ltd, 1954), chap. 1, Kindle.

[4]Bonhoeffer, *Life Together*, chap. 1.

[5]Jonathan Merritt, "America's Epidemic of Empty Churches," *The Atlantic*, November 25, 2018, www.theatlantic.com/ideas/archive/2018/11/what-should-america-do-its-empty -church-buildings/576592.

[6]Barna, "Signs of Decline & Hope Among Key Metrics of Faith," Barna: State of the Church 2020, March 4, 2020, www.barna.com/research/changing-state-of-the -church.

[7]Wendy Wang and Alyssa Elhage, "Here's Who Stopped Going to Church During the Pandemic," *Christianity Today*, January 20, 2022, www.christianitytoday.com /ct/2022/january-web-only/attendance-decline-covid-pandemic-church.html.

9. TRANSFORMING OUR DISCIPLESHIP ASSUMPTIONS

[1]Soong-Chan Rah, personal correspondence with author, May 26, 2020.

[2]Aaron Earls, "Small Churches Continue Growing—but in Number, Not Size," Lifeway Research, October 20, 2021, http://research.lifeway.com/2021/10/20/small-churches -continue-growing-but-in-number-not-size.

10. THE FOUR SPACES AND DISCIPLESHIP

[1] Joseph Myers, *The Search to Belong: Rethinking Intimacy, Community, and Small Groups* (Grand Rapids, MI: Zondervan, 2003), 22-24.

[2] Developed in the 1960s by Edward T. Hall, *The Hidden Dimension* (New York: Anchor Books, 1966), and popularized by Myers in *The Search to Belong*.

[3] Woodward, "Multiplying Discipleship Through the Four Spaces of Belonging," (The V3 Movement article, 2020), 74.

[4] Other grouping frameworks are also popular; for example, British anthropologist Robin Dunbar asserted that human beings can have five loved ones, fifteen good friends, fifty friends, and 150 meaningful contacts in their life; see "Dunbar's Number: Why We Can Only Maintain 150 Relationships," BBC, Future, October 1, 2019, www.bbc.com/future /article/20191001-dunbars-number-why-we-can-only-maintain-150-relationships. Another popular view is using Jesus' model of having three disciples in the inner circle, doing ministry with twelve disciples, and starting the church with the 120 at Pentecost (Acts 1:15); see Andy Crouch and Carey Nieuwhof, "The Breakdown of Trust, the Problem with Personalization and the Disruptions We'll Be Dealing with for the Rest of Our Lives," *Carey Nieuwhof Leadership Podcast*, June 28, 2022, ep. 503, www.careynieuwhof.com/episode503.

[5] Woodward, "Multiplying Discipleship," 5.

[6] Serenity Gibbons, "How Cohort-Based Learning Is Transforming Online Education," *Forbes*, December 17, 2021, www.forbes.com/sites/serenitygibbons/2021/12/17/how -cohort-based-learning-is-transforming-online-education.

[7] Dietrich Bonhoeffer, *The Cost of Discipleship* (New York: Touchstone, 1995), 59.

[8] Mark A. Maddix, "John Wesley's Small Groups: Models of Christian Community," Good Shepherd United Methodist Church, November 26, 2019, www.belonggsumc.com /john-wesleys-small-groups-models-of-christian-community.

[9] Stephen Nichols, "An Underground Seminary," *5 Minutes in Church History* (podcast), Ligonier, March 10, 2021, www.ligonier.org/podcasts/5-minutes-in-church-history -with-stephen-nichols/an-underground-seminary.

[10] Aaron Earls, "Small Churches Continue Growing—but in Number, Not Size," Lifeway Research, October 20, 2021, http://research.lifeway.com/2021/10/20/small-churches -continue-growing-but-in-number-not-size.

[11] Ed Stetzer and Eric Geiger, *Transformational Groups: Creating a New Scorecard for Groups*, (Nashville: B&H Publishing Group, 2014), chap. 1, Kindle.

[12] JR Woodward and Dan White Jr., *The Church as Movement: Starting and Sustaining Missional-Incarnational Communities* (Downers Grove, IL: InterVarsity Press, 2016), chap. 6, Kindle.

[13] The idea and first development of this differentiation between small groups and personal space came from Tim Catchim, though this is an adaptation from JR Woodward, "The Fundamentals of Discipleship" (The V3 Movement, curriculum for Year 2 cohort, September 2014), 6.

11. HURDLES TO DISCIPLESHIP

[1]National Trust for Canada, "National Trust Endangered Places List 2020," January 2021, https://nationaltrustcanada.ca/wp-content/uploads/2021/01/EPL-2020-Year-in-Review-Web-Posting-Final.pdf.

[2]Barna, "What Young Adults Say Is Missing from Church," November 13, 2019, www.barna.com/research/missing-church; "One in Three Practicing Christians Has Stopped Attending Church During COVID-19," Barna: State of the Church 2020, July 8, 2020, www.barna.com/research/new-sunday-morning-part-2.

[3]Ryan P. Burge, "Evangelicals Show No Decline, Despite Trump and Nones," *Christianity Today*, March 21, 2019, https://www.christianitytoday.com/news/2019/march/evangelical-nones-mainline-us-general-social-survey-gss.html.

[4]Amy Adkins, "Millennials: The Job-Hopping Generation," Gallup, May 11, 2016, www.gallup.com/workplace/231587/millennials-job-hopping-generation.aspx.

[5]Samantha Masunaga, "Millennials Want More Flexibility in Workplace Schedule, Survey Says," *Los Angeles Times*, May 29, 2015, www.latimes.com/business/la-fi-millennial-work-life-20150528-story.html.

[6]"Daring to be Vulnerable with Brené Brown," Earl E. Bakken Center for Spirituality & Healing, University of Minnesota, copyright 2016, www.takingcharge.csh.umn.edu/daring-be-vulnerable-brene-brown.

[7]Barna, "Children's Ministry is Crucial, But Its Impact is Hard to Measure" Barna Research, May 25, 2022, www.barna.com/research/childrens-ministry.

[8]Holly Catterton Allen and Christine Lawton Ross, *Intergenerational Christian Formation: Bringing the Whole Church Together in Ministry, Community and Worship* (Downers Grove, IL: InterVarsity Press, 2012), 17.

[9]Utilized in JR Woodward and Dan White Jr., *The Church as Movement: Starting and Sustaining Missional-Incarnational Communities* (Downers Grove, IL: InterVarsity Press, 2016), 228. As noted there, this unique grouping of the five Cs was developed by Tim Catchim.

[10]Dallas Willard, "Following Jesus and Living the Kingdom," Christianity + Renewal, May 2002, www.renovare.org/articles/living-in-the-kingdom.

12. DISCIPLESHIP IN CULTURE

[1]Rodney Stark, *The Rise Christianity: How the Obscure, Marginal Jesus Movement Became the Dominant Religious Force in the Western World in a Few Centuries* (San Francisco: Harper San Francisco, 1997), chap. 1, Kindle.

[2]Dorina Betz, "The 7 Mountains of Influence," YWAM Kosova, 2018, ywamkosova.com/the-7-mountains-of-influence; Roselie McDevitt and Joan Van Hise, "Influences in Ethical Dilemmas of Increasing Intensity," *Journal of Business Ethics* 40 (October 2022): 261-74.

[3]John Featherby, "What Are the 'Seven Spheres of Society'?" Shoremount, updated 2020, http://shoremount.kayako.com/article/43-what-are-the-seven-spheres-of-society.

[4]H. Richard Niebuhr, *Christ and Culture* (New York: Harper & Row 1951).

[5]Andy Crouch, *Culture Making* (Downers Grove, IL: InterVarsity Press, 2009), chap. 5, Kindle.

[6]Crouch, *Culture Making*, chap. 13, Kindle.

[7]The phrase "cultural mandate," often used interchangeably with "creation mandate," was popularized recently by Nancy Pearcey, *Total Truth: Liberating Christianity from Its Cultural Captivity* (Wheaton, IL: Crossway Books, 2004).

[8]Lesslie Newbigin, *A Word in Season* (Grand Rapids, MI: William B. Eerdmans, 1994), chap. 11, Kindle.

ABOUT THE AUTHOR

EUN K. STRAWSER, DO, is the covocational lead pastor of *Ma Ke Alo o* (which means "presence" in Hawaiian) non-denominational missional communities multiplying in Honolulu; a community physician at *Ke Ola Pono*; and an executive leader at the V3 Movement, the church-planting arm of the Baptist General Association of Virginia. Prior to transitioning to Hawaii, she served as adjunct professor of medicine at the Philadelphia College of Osteopathic Medicine and of African Studies at her alma mater, the University of Pennsylvania (where she and her husband served with InterVarsity Christian Fellowship) after finishing her Fulbright Scholarship at the University of Dar es Salaam. She and her husband, Steve, have three seriously amazing children.

www.centeringdiscipleship.com
Instagram @ekstrawser

Ma Ke Alo o (MKAO), Co-Lead Pastor
eun@mkao.community
www.mkao.community
Instagram @mkao.community

The V3 Movement, Movement Leader
eun@thev3movement.org
www.thev3movement.org
Instagram @thev3movement

Missio Alliance

and

InterVarsity Press

Missio Alliance has arisen in response to the shared voice of pastors and ministry leaders from across the landscape of North American Christianity for a new "space" of togetherness and reflection amid the issues and challenges facing the church in our day. We are united by a desire for a fresh expression of evangelical faith, one significantly informed by the global evangelical family. Lausanne's Cape Town Commitment, "A Confession of Faith and a Call to Action," provides an excellent guidepost for our ethos and aims.

In partnership with InterVarsity Press, we are pleased to offer a line of resources authored by a diverse range of theological practitioners. The resources in this series are selected based on the important way in which they address and embody these values, and thus, the unique contribution they offer in equipping Christian leaders for fuller and more faithful participation in God's mission.

Available Titles

missioalliance.org | twitter.com/missioalliance | facebook.com/missioalliance